D0654827

# MARRAKESH
## ENCOUNTER

**ALISON BING**

Marrakesh Encounter

**Published by Lonely Planet Publications Pty Ltd**
ABN 36 005 607 983

| | |
|---|---|
| **Australia** | Head Office, Locked Bag 1, Footscray, Vic 3011 |
| | ☎ 03 8379 8000  fax 03 8379 8111 |
| | talk2us@lonelyplanet.com.au |
| **USA** | 150 Linden St, Oakland, CA 94607 |
| | ☎ 510 893 8555 |
| | toll free 800 275 8555 |
| | fax 510 893 8572 |
| | info@lonelyplanet.com |
| **UK** | 2nd Fl, 186 City Rd |
| | London EC1V 2NT |
| | ☎ 020 7106 2100 fax 020 7106 2101 |
| | go@lonelyplanet.co.uk |

This title was commissioned in Lonely Planet's Melbourne office and produced by: **Commissioning Editors** Carolyn Boicos, Lucy Monie **Coordinating Editors** Charlotte Harrison, Jocelyn Harewood **Coordinating Cartographer** Julie Dodkins **Layout Designer** Jim Hsu **Assisting Editor** Jennifer Garrett **Assisting Cartographers** David Connolly, Diana Duggan, Wayne Murphy **Senior Editor** Sasha Baskett **Managing Cartographers** Shahara Ahmed, Adrian Persoglia **Cover Designer** Pepi Bluck **Project Manager** Rachel Imeson **Series Designers** Wendy Wright **Managing Layout Designer** Celia Wood **Thanks to** Geoff Howard, Quentin Frayne, Raphael Richards, Kerryn Burgess, Marg Toohey, Emma Gilmour, Stefanie Di Trocchio, Holly Alexander, Lisa Knights

**Cover photograph** Man at the Ensemble Artisanal, Hivernage, Doug McKinlay/LPI. **Internal photographs** All photographs by Lonely Planet Images, and by Marco Flavio Marinucci except p4, p6, p8, p18, p23, p28, p130 by Doug McKinlay.

All images are copyright of the photographers unless otherwise indicated. Many of the images in this guide are available for licensing from **Lonely Planet Images:** www.lonelyplanetimages.com.

ISBN 978 1 74104 787 5

Printed by Hang Tai Printing Company.
Printed in China.

# HOW TO USE THIS BOOK
## Colour-Coding & Maps

Colour-coding is used for symbols on maps and in the text that they relate to (eg all eating venues on the maps and in the text are given a green fork symbol). Each neighbourhood also gets its own colour, and this is used down the edge of the page and throughout that neighbourhood section.

Shaded yellow areas on the maps denote 'areas of interest' – for their historical significance, their attractive architecture or their great bars and restaurants. We encourage you to head to these areas and just start exploring!

## ALISON BING

Alison's first crush was on Sufi poet and whirling dervish honcho Rumi, after visiting his shrine in Turkey as a five year old. Though her own career as a dervish didn't quite pan out, she studied Islamic art, architecture and political economy at the American University in Cairo and Bryn Mawr College. Alison also holds a masters degree from the Fletcher School of Law and Diplomacy, a programme of Tufts and Harvard Universities – respectable diplomatic credentials she regularly undermines with opinionated art, food and culture commentary for newspapers, magazines and radio.

## ALISON'S THANKS

*Shukran bezzef* (many thanks) to editorial *maâlems* (experts) Marg Toohey, Carolyn Boicos, Lucy Monie and Holly Alexander for making this project possible; to project mavens Charlotte Harrison, Rachel Imeson and Jennifer Garrett for making it snappy; and to dauntless cartographers Shahara Ahmed and Julie Dodkins, who make 3000 *derbs* (winding alleys) somehow seem doable.

*Allah yhrem waldikum* (blessings upon your parents) to Marrakesh experts Souad Boudeiry, Saïda Chab, Meryanne Loum-Martin, Mohamed Nour and Ben Azzouz Said. *Tbarkallalek* (congratulations on your accomplishment) to Marco Flavio Marinucci for his magnificent photos capturing the warmth, humour, creativity and splendours of Marrakesh. To the people of Marrakesh who make it so: *Allah ykhlef*, may your many kindnesses be returned to you tenfold.

## THE PHOTOGRAPHER

Born and raised in Rome, where he trained as a fine artist, Marco Flavio Marinucci has lugged camera equipment from Japan to Morocco in pursuit of the perfect shot. When not obsessively photographing Marrakshi mint sellers, Marco divides his time between Proceno, Italy, and San Francisco, where he stalks local farmers markets for his weekly food photo blog (www.cookhereandnow.com).

**Our readers** Many thanks to the travellers who wrote to us with helpful hints, useful advice and interesting anecdotes. Bronny Bennett, Sherylene Kohiti.

It's never a chore, shopping at this small establishment that's like many found in the backstreets

# CONTENTS

# THIS IS MARRAKESH

Within minutes of arrival in Marrakesh's Medina (Old City) you'll learn a new word: 'Balek!' Roughly, 'Move it or lose it, donkey coming through!'

Donkey carts may not inspire the same adrenaline-rushing alertness as careening Vespas loaded with oranges, taxi drivers who mistake their Fiats for Formula Ones, and carpet sellers in hot pursuit of customers with their absolute last price. But once you glimpse the carts painted with good-luck symbols hurtling headlong through narrow souqs (covered market streets), you too will leap to the sidelines and watch in awe as Marrakesh rushes ahead by all available means.

Where is the city headed in such a hurry? Marrakesh has a hot date – with you actually. King Mohammed VI proclaimed that by 2010 Morocco will welcome 10 million visitors, with Marrakesh as the main point of entry. Since in just four days a traveller may spend about £850, the average yearly salary for a Moroccan, every visitor is a VIP in Marrakesh. Luckily, showing guests a good time comes readily to the *bahja*, or joyous ones, as Marrakshis are known. The Djemaa el-Fna has enchanted visitors for a millennium, with its chorus of 100 chefs singing their own praises, Gnaoua musicians banging out funky freedom songs on *ginbris* (two-stringed banjos) and potion-sellers' chants promising cures for rheumatism and heartbreak. Guests get the royal treatment in traditional hammams (bathhouses) and authentic riads, elegant mud-brick courtyard mansions that make the Medina a Unesco World Heritage Site.

The Pink City promises a rosier future for Moroccans, 40% of whom subsist below the poverty line, because many more visitors are seeking environmentally smart, culturally enriching travel options. So ecotourism is set to take off here. And not a moment too soon: this close to the Sahara global warming is no joke, and golf courses, water parks and dune buggies severely strain Morocco's resources. But with its traditions of organic cuisine, handicrafts, naturally cool mud-brick architecture and, yes, environmentally friendly donkey carts, modern-medieval Marrakesh could lead the way to the future. *Balek!*

**Top left** Belly dancers entertain at restaurants and night spots **Top right** Ancient Berber symbols feature in this design at Ministero del Gusto (p102) **Bottom** One of the many colourful food stalls (p72) set up each afternoon on the Djemaa el-Fna

One of the rooms at the Théâtre Royal (p60) in Nouvelle Ville

# >1 DJEMAA EL-FNA

**WATCH NONSTOP DRAMA IN THE DJEMAA EL-FNA**

PT Barnum was bluffing when he called his circus 'the greatest show on earth'; that title has belonged to the Djemaa el-Fna for almost a millennium. The hoopla and *halqa* (street theatre) has been nonstop here ever since this plaza was used for public executions in about 1050 – hence its name, which means 'assembly of the dead'.

The curtain goes up on the Djemaa el-Fna around 9am, when juice vendors haul in carts loaded with oranges, potion purveyors and henna tattoo artists set up shop under umbrellas, and pedestrians begin their dance dodging motor scooters and donkey carts. Water sellers in fringed hats lug their metal dispensers around the plaza as though they haven't heard of bottled water, gamely pausing to pose for photos for a few dirhams.

The second act begins in the afternoon, when the entertainers arrive. Snake charmers strike up oboe numbers that may sound dissonant to humans, but are apparently irresistible club tunes among the serpent set. Like all-male cheerleader squads, track-suited acrobats attempt to rouse afternoon café crowds with back flips and human pyramids. But Gnaoua musicians always steal the show with syncopated songs heavy on drums and castanets; working

themselves and their audience into an ecstatic trance that gets fez tassels spinning, toes tapping and everyone grinning. As always in the Djemaa, applause and tips in any amount keep the good vibes and encores coming.

When evening arrives, storytellers spellbind crowds with legends told in Arabic and dramatic gestures that need no translation. Astrologers, healers and cross-dressing belly dancers move to the periphery as some 100 food stalls set up shop and barbecue smoke rises from the Djemaa like dry ice in preparation for the evening's grande finale. The reviews are in: Unesco declared the Djemaa el-Fna a Masterpiece of World Heritage in 2001.

See also p68 and p70.

---

### CAMEO APPEARANCES

Stick around and you might catch a command performance by special guest stars in the Djemaa:

> Scribes who will read, write and notarise Dear John letters, no questions asked.
> Dentists with pointy pliers and a jar of teeth…enough said.
> Glass eaters, apparently here to entertain and keep the dentists in business.
> Fire swallowers who make glass and *harissa* hot sauce seem digestible by comparison.

---

HIGHLIGHTS

# >2 SOUQS

## GET LOST AND FIND TREASURES IN THE SOUQS:
## THE ULTIMATE URBAN LABYRINTH

You haven't really been to Marrakesh until you've gotten lost in these covered markets. Slow down and look around: when rays of sunlight through the palm-frond roof illuminate a lute maker at work, you've found the Instrument-makers' Souq (Souq Kimakhine), and if you glimpse sparks flying as old bicycle parts are refashioned into lanterns, Souq Haddadine (Blacksmiths' Souq) has found you. Souq Sebbaghine (Dyers' Souq) is the most picturesque, with skeins of freshly dyed saffron and vermillion wool hung to dry against Marrakshi pink walls and Saharan blue skies.

But don't stop there: dive into the labyrinthine *qissaria* (covered market) between Souq Smata (Slipper Souq) and Souq Semmarine (Leather Souq), where artisans in cubbyhole workshops fashion next season's It Bag using tools and techniques inherited from great-great-grandparents. From morning to evening, this area buzzes with the sounds of handiwork in progress and artisans calling out greetings to passers-by in five languages. Anyone who stops by is promptly given a nickname – divulge your favourite footballer or hobby, and there you have it – and return customers are treated to warm greetings and hot tea.

Pause for unexpected beauty and banter often, because what are the chances you'll come this way again? Even locals and compass-equipped cartographers lose their way in millennia-old Medina

### TOP FIVE SOUQ JOKES

Multilingual Marrakshi vendors make jokes of any overheard word, and no trip to the souqs would be complete without hearing one of these groaners:

> 'Berber whiskey': mint tea
> 'Air-conditioned shoes': raffia slippers
> 'Berber 4x4': donkey cart
> '30 camels': the going rate for a dowry; hold out for a Vespa
> 'Berber Adidas': rubber-soled *babouches* (slippers)

streets flanked by some 3000 *derbs* (winding alleys), which predate
city planning and defy satellite mapping. You could hire a guide, but
you'd be missing most of the fun and all the deals – odds are your
guide is related to the shopkeeper or gets a commission. Go it alone
instead, and never be too proud to bow gracefully out of a bargaining session or backtrack the way you came. Think of the souqs as the
Bermuda Triangle of shopping: if you emerge blinking in the sunlight
of the Djemaa el-Fna clutching fewer than five shopping bags, a
victorious glass of orange juice is in order.

See also p81.

# >3 ALI BEN YOUSSEF MEDERSA

## GET A HIGHER EDUCATION IN MOROCCAN ARTISTRY AT ALI BEN YOUSSEF MEDERSA

Insiders say Marrakesh's palaces can't compare with its wonders wrought for the glory of God. While local mosques and *zaouias* (saint shrines) are closed to non-Muslims, you can see what the insiders mean at this medersa (Quranic school). Founded in the 14th century under the Merenids, the Ali ben Youssef Medersa was once the largest in North Africa and remains one of the most splendid. Look up in the entry hall, and admire intricately carved cedar cupolas and *mashrabiyya* (wooden-lattice screen) balconies. To add an ahh to that ooh, enter the medersa's courtyard. The arcaded cloisters are Hispano-Moresque wonders of five-colour, high-lustre *zellij* (mosaic) and ingenious Iraqi-style Kufic stucco, with letters intertwined in leaves and knots. Just…wow. Or as the medersa's students might say: *Allahuakbar* (God is great).

Facing stiff competition from medersas in Fez, the school closed in 1962. But in its heyday, up to 900 students lived in the 130 dorm rooms here – and shared one bathroom. Upstairs, a 3-sq-metre dorm room overlooking the courtyard shows how students lived, with a sleeping mat, writing implements, a Quran bookstand and a hotplate. Just like your university days minus the partying, and with even more prayers come exam time.

See also p80.

## >4 SAADIAN TOMBS

**REVISIT MARRAKESH'S GOLDEN AGE AT SAADIAN TOMBS**

Who says you can't take it with you? Surely not 16th-century Saadian Sultan Ahmed el-Mansour el-Dahbi, known as 'The Victorious' for defeating Portuguese foes of the Sudan, and as 'The Golden' for cheating customers with exorbitant sugar prices. With his spoils, this Marrakshi Midas gilded the lavish stucco-and-marble Chamber of the Twelve Pillars to make it a suitably glorious final resting place.

The sultan was quite the family man, numerically speaking, and kept his many wives, relatives, children and servants close even in death – hence the 170-plus tombs in this compound. The small *zellij* tombs in the gardens are for wives, trusty Jewish councillors and lesser relations, while the alpha-male Saadian princes are interred in the Chamber of the Three Niches. The sultan's mother has her own mausoleum, vigilantly guarded by stray cats in the courtyard.

El-Mansour died in splendour in 1603, but a scant few decades later Alawite Sultan Moulay Ismail walled up the Saadian Tombs to keep his predecessors out of sight and mind. Accessible only through a small passage in the Kasbah Mosque, the tombs were neglected by all except the storks until aerial photography exposed them in 1917.

See also p111.

HIGHLIGHTS

# >5 KOUTOUBIA MINARET

## HEAR THE KOUTOUBIA'S MELODIC MUEZZIN RISE ABOVE THE HAWKERS' HUBBUB

Five times a day, one voice rises above the Djemaa din for the adhan, or call to prayer: that's the muezzin atop the Koutoubia Minaret calling the faithful in all four cardinal directions, so no Marrakshi can claim to have missed a reminder of the *salah* (five daily prayers). Other muezzin may be less than punctual, shout out a sura (Quranic verse), or clear their throats like chain smokers, but not at the Koutoubia: the entire sura flows with impeccable syllabic accents and an unbroken melody from beginning to end.

The Koutoubia Minaret is the ultimate Marrakshi muezzin gig. This 12th-century, 70m-high tower is the architectural prototype for Seville's La Giralda and Rabat's Tour Hassan, and it's a monumental cheat sheet of Moorish ornament: scalloped keystone arches, jagged merlons (crenulations) and mathematically pleasing proportions. Originally the minaret was sheathed in Marrakshi pinkish plaster, but experts opted to preserve its exposed stone and time-tested character in its 1990s restoration. The Koutoubia mosque is off limits to non-Muslims, but the gardens are fair game, and a prime location to hear the Koutoubia adhan up close.

See also p70.

## >6 BAHIA PALACE

### PREPARE TO BE FLOORED BY THE WOODWORKED CEILINGS AT BAHIA PALACE

Imagine what you could build with Morocco's top artisans at your service for 14 years, and here you have it. *La Bahia* (The Beautiful) boasts floor-to-ceiling decoration begun by Grand Vizier Si Moussa in the 1860s, and further embellished from 1894 to 1900 by slave-turned-vizier Abu 'Bou' Ahmed. The painted, gilded, inlaid woodwork ceilings still have the intended effect of awing crowds, while the carved stucco is cleverly slanted downward to meet the gaze. Detractors sniff that the polychrome *zellij* could be fitted together more tightly, but we'd like to see them try.

Though only a portion of the palace's 8 hectares and 150 rooms is open to the public, you can see the unfurnished, opulently ornamented harem that once housed Bou Ahmed's four wives and 24 concubines and the grand Court of Honour, once packed with people begging for the despot's mercy. Warlord Madani Glaoui entertained European friends and tortured Moroccan enemies here from 1908 to 1911, until his French guests booted their host out and established the Protectorate's *résident-généraux* here. Mohammed VI is more careful about his choice of royal guests, who range from dignitaries to rapper Sean 'Diddy' Combs.

See also p108.

# >7 HAMMAMS

## GET STEAM CLEANED, ROUGHED UP AND PLASTERED WITH MUD IN A TRADITIONAL HAMMAM

Slimed, roughed up, and slathered in mud: what sounds like very naughty playground behaviour is actually a glorious Moroccan spa treatment. Keeping your skin fresh and dewy this close to the Sahara requires extreme measures, and Berbers have stuck to more or less the same beauty regimen for a millennium. In a steamy domed hammam (bathhouse), a *tebbaya* (bath attendant) slathers your skin with slippery *savon noir*, black soap made with palm and olive oil plus pore-cleansing essential oils. When the going gets rough, the rough get thoroughly scrubbed with an exfoliating *kessa* (rough-textured glove). Many layers of shed dead skin later – you'll be surprised and slightly aghast to see just how much was clogging your pores – you're ready for a soothing *rhassoul* (mud scalp rub) before a fragrant orange-flower water rinse and a coating of emollient argan oil.

Does this regime actually work? Maybe too well: back in the 7th century, Ummayad caliphs took a particular shine to Berber women, and drafted many into their royal harems. So as you emerge from the hammam soft, pliable and glowing, be thankful those pesky Ummayads were driven out of Berber territory by warrior Queen al-Kahina – and don't forget to reapply your SPF30.

See also p143.

# >8 JARDIN MAJORELLE

**STRIKE A POSE AMID HIGH-FASHION CACTI IN YVES SAINT LAURENT'S JARDIN MAJORELLE**

Some people send thank-you cards, but Yves Saint Laurent gave this spectacular garden as a token of appreciation to the city that adopted him in 1964 after a sequence of events that included, in rather unfortunate order: launching hippie fashion; fame as a ground-breaking gay icon; and an obligatory stint in the French military.

Saint Laurent and his partner Pierre Bergère bought the garden with its Art Deco villa, now the Museum of Islamic Arts, from acclaimed landscape painter Jacques Majorelle. In 1924 Majorelle complemented his collection of rare flora with vivid touches of colour for a look that remains shockingly contemporary: fuchsia bougainvillea explodes from Day-Glo yellow terracotta planters, cacti lean against cobalt-blue plaster walls like slouching rock stars, and goldfish flash neon orange in pale-green reflecting pools.

To best appreciate Majorelle's artistic accomplishment, visit at high noon or on a sweltering summer's day, when the place is like a desert mirage. The blue and green hues seem to quench your thirst, bamboo thickets rustle in the slightest breeze, and turtles lazing around under drawbridges set a fine example.

See also p41.

# >9 DAR SI SAID

**EXPLORE MOROCCAN ARTS AND FIND HOME DÉCOR INSPIRATION AT THE SUBLIME DAR SI SAID**

Historical rumour has it that Grand Vizier 'Bou' Ahmed's brother Si Said wasn't the brightest dirham in the royal treasury, but judging by his palace, he might've been craftier than anyone suspected. While 'Bou' Ahmed demanded a rush job on the Bahia Palace, Si Said gave his *maâlems* (master craftspeople) time to refine their work. Today the Bahia is a marvel of glitz with the occasional slapdash slip, but Dar Si Said is a model of restrained 19th-century elegance. Si Said's artisans outdid themselves in the upstairs wedding chamber, covering the walls, musicians' balconies and ceiling with a truly joyous profusion of floral ornament – you can almost hear the women ululating.

The Dar Si Said also features a well-curated selection of southern Moroccan arts with like items grouped together, so visitors can appreciate Moroccan artisans' ingenious variations on kohl (eyeliner) bottles and inlaid daggers. The carved wooden doors on display are similar in style but always distinct in detail, so that you can almost imagine the family living behind each one, and the 3rd-floor display of ancient kitchen utensils in the former *douira* (kitchen) will give you a new appreciation of food processors.

See also p109.

# >10 MOROCCAN FEASTS

## FEAST IN STYLE AT A MULTICOURSE MOROCCAN *DIFFA*

When mere dinner won't do, Moroccans celebrate with a proper *diffa* (feast). Seasonal delicacies are served family style from shared platters, and guests are cajoled into eating with a good-humoured insistence that would do your grandmother proud. In restaurants and at Moroccan weddings and family functions, the feeding frenzy is often punctuated with conversation and live musical entertainment.

The desired result is happy taste buds, harmony among humankind and the sleep of the dead. But be warned: some palace restaurants attempt to distract diners from their dismal cafeteria-style fare with laser shows, belly dancers helpfully simulating digestion and over-the-top décor straight out of a genie's bottle. Accept no imitations for the real meal deal, which includes three to five courses cooked to order and perfection, whether fixed-price or à la carte.

A daring *diffa* begins with a starter of three to seven cooked salads ranging from slow-cooked smoky eggplant to tangy-sweet beets, possibly followed by legendary Moroccan *bastilla* (pigeon pie). Next up: succulent meats barbecued, slow-roasted, and/or served dissolving into bubbling, delicate sauces flavoured with *smen* (seasoned clarified butter). Then comes fluffy conical couscous piled with seasonal vegetables and scented with saffron. Save room for dessert, which could be simple cinnamon-laced oranges or kingly dessert *bastilla* (flaky pastry with rich cream and almonds). Afterwards, bow down to the *dada* (cook) – if you still can.

See also p134.

# >11 MUSÉE DE MARRAKESH

## UNCOVER PALACE INTRIGUES AMONG THE TREASURES AT MUSÉE DE MARRAKESH

If these 19th-century palace walls could talk, they'd dish out dirt on Queen Victoria and Mehdi Mnebhi, minister of defence during the brief, troubled 1894–1908 reign of Sultan Moulay Abdelaziz. While Minister Mnebhi was busy schmoozing European royals and receiving a medal from Queen Victoria, sneaky England was secretly conspiring with France and Spain to carve up North Africa. When the sultan ceded control to France and Spain, Mnebhi beat a hasty retreat to Tangiers, and Anglophile autocrat Pasha Glaoui snatched this palace. After Independence, it was seized by the state and became Marrakesh's first girls' school in 1965.

Today the pristine palace is a haven of serenity, elegantly restored by the Omar Benjelloun Foundation. The arcaded inner courtyard is flanked by traditional arts displays, including recent travelling shows of High Atlas carpets and Moroccan Jewish artefacts. Also of interest is the original hammam, with several chambers to accommodate varying needs for heat, from the vaguely arthritic to the seriously hung-over. But there's still plenty of fodder for local gossip in the lovely green and white *douira* gallery, which incongruously exhibits melting-face surrealism, kitschy clown paintings and other unfortunate examples of European modern art.

See also p82.

# >MARRAKESH DIARY

You'll never need an excuse for a party in the home of the *bahja* (joyous ones).
Join a Gnaoua *leila* (trance jam session) any night in the Djemaa el-Fna, where
cross-dressing belly dancers invite partners with playful flicks of their veils.
Lately savvy club promoters have organised shindigs in other outdoor venues,
including lounge music with Bryan Ferry at the Badi Palace (www.purodesert
lounge.com). Official occasions such as the annual film festival or marathon
(find listings in French at www.marrakechpocket.com and www.maghrebarts
.ma) are inevitably upstaged by raucous sing-along Bollywood screenings and
children cheering themselves hoarse for hometown favourite runners.

Entry to the Ali ben Youssef Medersa (p80), a centre of Quranic learning in the 14th century

MARRAKESH DIARY

# JANUARY

## Marathon of Marrakesh
www.marathon-marrakech.com
Run like there's a carpet seller after you from the Djemaa to the Palmeraie and back.

# MARCH

## Rencontres Musicales de Marrakech
www.maghrebarts.ma
Classical groupies pack the Théâtre Royal for performances ranging from Arab-Andalusian favourites to Beethoven.

Marrakesh marathon training in the Palmeraie

# APRIL

## Aicha des Gazelles
www.rallyeaichadesgazelles.com
This gazelle will run you down: women race offroad through the Sahara to Essaouira.

## Jardin'Art Garden Festival
www.jardinsdumaroc.com/festival
The Pink City goes green with living sculptures, sustainability forums and Cyberpark concerts on the second weekend in April.

## Essaouira Alizés (Trade Winds) Classical Music Festival
www.alizesfestival.com
The third weekend in April sees 20 concerts in four days, with interfaith chants, original compositions and Mozart megahits.

# MAY

## Berber Marathon
www.runningclubmaroc.com
An uphill battle: hardy runners take on the High Atlas mountains near Oukaimeden.

# JUNE

## Essaouira Gnaoua Music Festival
www.festival-gnaoua.co.ma
Surfers, Sufis, Moroccan Rastas and roots musicologists get funky with Gnaoua and pan-African music at North Africa's grooviest music festival on the third weekend in June.

Tuning up in the Djemaa el-Fna

# JULY

## Marrakesh Festival of Popular Arts

www.marrakechfestival.com

The only thing hotter than Marrakesh in July is this free-form folk fest held on the first weekend in July. Berber musicians, dancers and street performers from around the country pour into Marrakesh to thrill the masses, with impromptu performance marathons in the Djemaa that easily rival officially scheduled international folk acts.

# SEPTEMBER

## Imilchil Marriage Festival

Intense flirting and negotiation ensue at this Middle Atlas *moussem* (celebration), where women come from miles around to harvest husbands. Date depends on harvest schedule.

# DECEMBER

## Marrakesh International Film Festival

www.festival-marrakech.com

Sundance seems staid compared with this eclectic showcase of independent and postcolonial film that includes movies shot in Morocco. Hollywood glitterati such as Martin Scorsese, Susan Sarandon and 2006 jury president Roman Polanski are overshadowed by literal red-carpet royalty and raucous Bollywood screenings in the Djemaa. On the first or second weekend in December.

### PUBLIC HOLIDAYS

While state holidays are held on the same date each year, the dates of religious holidays change each year in accordance with the lunar Hejira calendar. See p164 for a list of public holiday dates for 2008 and 2009.

# >ITINERARIES

Golden light in Musée de Marrakesh's covered courtyard (p82)

# ITINERARIES

## DAY ONE

Get juiced on freshly squeezed OJ in the Djemaa el-Fna (p70) and rush headlong into the souqs along Rue el-Mouassine, past Souq Sebbaghine (Dyers' Souq) toward Rahba Qedima (p83) and herbalists' special offers of 'Berber Viagara' (galanga). Compare wares you've seen in the souqs with examples of prime craftsmanship at the Musée de Marrakesh (p82), and see how your alma mater stacks up against the glorious Ali ben Youssef Medersa (p80). Follow your rumbling stomach toward the smell of baking bread at the Souq el-Fassi *farnatchi* (oven; p80) or feast in style at Le Foundouk (p87). Dodge a dozen carpet sellers on your way back to the Djemaa and congratulations: you've got the hang of Marrakesh.

## DAY TWO

Your Marrakshi romance begins at Dar Si Said (p109), where the exuberantly painted wedding chamber may inspire ululation. Down Riad Zitoun el-Jedid, the bodaciously ornamented Bahia Palace (p108) harem may make you rethink both décor and monogamy. For lunch, enjoy a tagine hot off the burner in Restaurant Place des Ferblantiers (p114) or indulge in the haute-cuisine version at elegant Tangia (p115). Peek into the Badi Palace (p108) for storks' love nests and the miraculous marquetry of the Koutoubia Minbar (p109), then pay your respects to the sultan who left his wives out in the rain at the Saadian Tombs (p111). Unwind in the steamy Sultana Spa (p116) or with a candlelit bath for two at Les Bains de Marrakesh (p115), and let Marrakesh work its charms.

## LAZY DAY

Roll out of your riad around noon and grab a taxi to Jardin Majorelle (p41), where towering cacti and vibrant colours awaken the senses. Take a taxi to a late lunch at Al Fassia (p47), then hit the gallery scene along Rue de Yougoslavie en route to Rue de la Liberté for boutique-browsing and cappuccino at mod Kechmara (p50). Mosey down Ave Mohammed V to watch artisans at work at Ensemble Artisanal (p40), and stop to smell the roses and send insincere 'wish you were here' emails to coworkers at Cyberpark (p37). Dinner at La Table du Marché (p50) is only a couple of blocks from drinks at Jad Mahal (p57) and groovy DJs at Le Comptoir (p55).

**Top left** The Koutoubia mosque and gardens (p70) **Top right** Things are looking up at the Bahia Palace (p108) **Bottom** Still made by hand at the Ensemble Artisanal (p40) where you can watch the artisans at work

## HOT SUMMER DAY

Take your cue from the empty streets and get out of town. Take a mountain-stream hike in cool, picturesque Imlil (p146) then stop at Dar Taliba (see boxed text, p157) for a refreshing Berber tea and visit to the nonprofit herb garden and school (donations appreciated and used wisely). Or take a cooking class in the Palmeraie at Jnane Tamsna (p66). If you can't stand the heat, you can get out of the kitchen and dive into one of four pools amid organic gardens – and fight global warming by donating to a palm-tree-planting programme (see boxed text, p157).

## DURING RAMADAN

Early risers carbo-load before dawn with the faithful, then stock up on lunch supplies in the early-morning rush on the souqs or the Marché Municipale (p46). Hit the sights before returning to the riad for a nap and discreet lunch. Slackers can sleep late without missing much, and eat in at the riad before an afternoon photo safari in atmospherically deserted streets and monuments. Near dusk the buzz in the souqs is palpable, as dates, *harira* (lentil soup) and *chebbakia* (honey pastry) are readied for the *iftar* (break-fast) rush. At sundown the feasting begins, and when the

When the sun sets, fasting for Ramadan ends with a feast of dates in the souqs

## FORWARD PLANNING

**Three weeks before you go** Make riad reservations (p117), book classes in Moroccan cooking or crafts (see boxed text, p66) and trekking excursions in the High Atlas – your riad can probably do it for you – and start mastering Moroccan Arabic pleasantries for smiles and sweet deals in the souqs (p82).

**One week before you go** Book a hammam (p143) and tune into Moroccan radio online at www.maroc.net/rc to loosen up those hips. Organise a *diffa* (feast; p21) to work off on the dance floor.

**The day before you go** Check out what's making Moroccan headlines at www.friends ofmorocco.org and get the inside scoop from Moroccan author/blogger Laila Lalami at www.lailalalami.com/blog/archives/cat_all_things_moroccan.html. Start working up an appetite now for your feast – a half marathon should do the trick.

main meal is served around 10pm, kids amped on sweets have the run of the streets and the Djemaa (p70) is packed with revellers. *Ramadan Mubarak!* (Happy Ramadan!)

## FOR FREE

Breakfast is complimentary at most riads, so fuel up before you brave the souqs, where you'll be assured constantly that 'looking is free' by vendors parading temptations before you. Check out the art show at Dar Chérifa (p98) en route to the Mouassine Fountain (p99), where neighbourhood gossip flows freely, then check out Fondouqs (p98) for glimpses of artisans at work without the sales pressure. Ensemble Artisanal (p40) offers an even closer look at crafts in progress before you hit the contemporary Moroccan art circuit at Galerie Ré (p40), Gallerie Noir Sur Blanc (p40) and Matisse Art Gallery (p41). Festivals mean free street entertainment and unbeatable people-watching – but you can always get free and funky in the Djemaa (p70) with Gnaoua musicians, whose winsome ways may convince you to part with cash for tips.

>NEIGHBOURHOODS

Past meets future: welcome to Marrakesh

# NEIGHBOURHOODS

Urban legends have been made in Marrakesh for a millennium. Nights of decadence and music once left Nouvelle Ville hotel floors littered with Rolling Stones and Beatles and parts of Led Zeppelin.

Writers and Bohemians headed to the Medina for enlightenment and *kif* (hashish), coming away with inspiration for books such as *Hideous Kinky* and *Naked Lunch*. Today, designers from Yves Saint Laurent to Jean Paul Gaultier call the Nouvelle Ville home. You might bump into Paul McCartney near his Palmeraie villa or meet Kate Moss, Iman or Naomi Campbell scouring the souqs for kaftans. Even Marrakesh's ancient monuments stay current: yes, that was Brangelina sipping mint tea in the Djemaa, Bryan Ferry introducing Badi Palace storks to lounge music, and rapper Sean 'Diddy' Combs dining with Mohammed VI at the Bahia Palace.

Travellers' tales usually revolve around the Djemaa el-Fna that serves as a stage for a Unesco-honoured ensemble of storytellers, cross-dressing belly dancers, snake charmers and potion sellers. On the north side of the Djemaa el-Fna, souq traders beckon with siren calls of 'Come in…just look…some tea?' East is Derb Debachi, a labyrinth of *derbs* (winding alleys). To the west is the venerable Mouassine, with its stately riads (mud-brick courtyard mansions). North is Bab Doukkala and Dar el-Bacha, once home to Marrakesh's dread despot but now a friendly neighbourhood of riads, hammams and a bustling food souq. Meanwhile, south of the Djemaa el-Fna lie the Riads Zitoun, lined with artisans' showplaces and spectacular palaces. Holding down the fort further south is the royal Kasbah, containing the king's official palace and the Saadian Tombs.

The plot thickens in the Nouvelle Ville (New City), created in 1912 for French colonial elites and now a prime spot to mingle with chic Marrakshis at sidewalk cafés, Art Deco villa restaurants and local designer boutiques. The most happening Nouvelle Ville nightclubs and bars are in Guéliz (north of the Medina) and the swanky hotels of Hivernage (west of the Medina). The stylish latecomer to the Marrakesh party is Palmeraie, the nouveau-riche oasis and celebrity haunt 5km east of town.

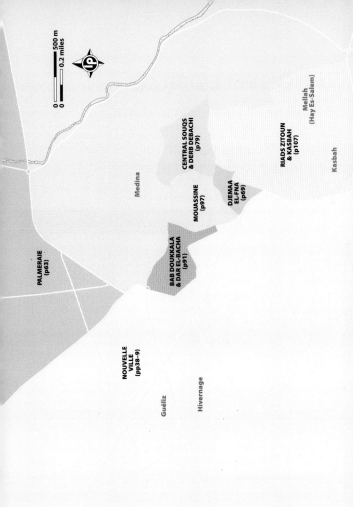

PALMERAIE (p63)

NOUVELLE VILLE (pp38–9)

Guéliz

Hivernage

Medina

BAB DOUKKALA & DAR EL-BACHA (p91)

MOUASSINE (p97)

CENTRAL SOUQS & DERB DEBACHI (p79)

DJEMAA EL-FNA (p69)

RIADS ZITOUN & KASBAH (p107)

Mellah (Hay Es-Salem)

Kasbah

0        500 m
0        0.2 miles

# > NOUVELLE VILLE

When the French set up shop in their 'New City' in 1912, they brought all the comforts of home: wide boulevards, garden villas, French bistros, and inescapable roundabouts. Independent-minded Moroccans kicked the French colonial government to the boulevard kerb in 1956, but wisely kept a few of the better bistros – and less prudently, retained the baffling roundabouts. More radical changes have occurred in recent years, with the boom in travel and a new Marrakshi middle class. Hivernage villas have been replaced by fancy hotels and, with the outstanding exception

# NOUVELLE VILLE

## ◉ SEE

## ⬟ SHOP

## 🍴 EAT

## 🍷 DRINK

## ★ PLAY

Please see over for map

Hanging out in Cyberpark

of the Jardin Majorelle and Guéliz, gardens have been mostly filled in with townhouses and apartments. But it's hard to bemoan such bygone glories, especially with your mouth full at tasty new Nouvelle Ville restaurants and patisseries. Sleeping seems overrated in hot spot–filled Hivernage, fuelled with espresso from Guéliz cafés. And in the past decade, the imported culture of Guéliz has been upgraded with home-grown galleries and boutiques showcasing Moroccan artists and designers, a grand royal theatre and a literary café. The Nouvelle Ville never looked so new.

## SEE
### CYBERPARK
**Ave Mohammed V, near Bab Nkob;
9am-7pm;**

Tiptoe through the tulips to check email at the Cyberpark, an 8-hectare royal garden dating from about 1700 that now offers free wi-fi. The paths are lined with orange trees, palms and internet

## Map labels

**To Lhasnaoui Rent (20m)**

**To Sidi Ghanem (2km)**

**To Niagara (100m)**

Jardin Majorelle

5

KNK La Kasbah Mutérik

Rue Khalid ben el-Oualid

NOUVELLE VILLE

Rue Ibn Toumert

Gendarmerie Royale

23

38

13

Ave Moulay Abdallah

Ave Yacoub el-Mansour

Rue Souria

Rue el-Imam Malik

Rue Sebou

Ave des Nations Unies

Ave Mohammed V

Rue Yaoula el-Matin

44

53

Rue Oum Errabia

10

4

Mosque

Place du 16 Novembre

Rue Ouadi

Rue el-Oualid Pasha

Rue Loubnan

9

Royal Air Maroc

24

36

Hôtel du Pacha

Crédit du Maroc

Rue Mansour Eddahbi

31

30

18

40

59

46

12

32

41

Rue Tariq Ibn Ziad

Bethel Synagogue

Rue de la Liberté

43

37

35

Rue de Yougoslavie

Rue Mauritanie

Hospital Ibn Tofail

Rue Abdelouahad Derraq

Rue Ibn Sina

Rue Moulay Ali

Rue Ibn Aïcha

Rue Ibn Zaïdoun

42

21 19

Budget

Polyclinique du Sud

Place Abdel Moumen ben Ali

GUÉLIZ

Sea Background

Ave Moulay Rachid

Rue el-Hassan ben N'Barek

29

Rue Mohammed el-Beqal

Guéliz CTM Office

39

Askmy Café

20

52

54

7

Main Train Station

50

**Ave Mohammed V**

**Ave Mohammed Abdelkrim el-Khattabi**

**Ave de France**

Blvd Mohammed VI

Zerktouni

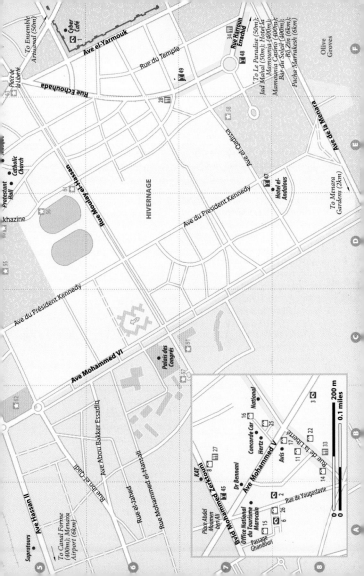

Olive
Groves

To Ensemble
Artisanal (50m)

Cyber
Café

Ave el-Yarmouk

Rue du Temple

Rue Echohada

Rue de Harroun
Errachid

To Le Paradise (50m);
Jad Mahal (50m); Hotel la
Mamounia (400m);
Mamounia Casino (400m);
Bar-da Soleil (400m);
BÔ Zin (6km);
Pacha Marrakesh (6km)

Place de
la Liberté

HIVERNAGE

Rue Moulay el-Hassan

Ave el-Oadssa

Hôtel el-
Andalous

Catholic
Church

Protestant
Hall

khazine

Ave du Président Kennedy

Ave du Président Kennedy

To Menara
Gardens (2km)

Ave de la Menara

Ave du Président Kennedy

Ave Mohammed VI

Palais des
Congrés

Ave Hassan II

Ave Abou Bakter Essadiq

Rue Ibn Aïcha

Rue el-Jahed

Rue Mohammed el-Hansali

Supratours

To Canal Forme
(400m); Menara
Airport (6km)

Place Abdel
Moumen
ben Ali

Office National
du Tourisme
Marocain

Bvd Mohammed Zerktouni

KAY

Dr Bennani

Concorde Car

Hertz

Avis

National

Ave Mohammed V

Rue de la Liberté

Rue de Yougoslavie

Passage
Ghandouri

0          200 m
0          0.1 miles

kiosks – wait your turn on benches filled with teenagers and nervous online daters.

## � ENSEMBLE ARTISANAL

☎ 024 443503; Ave Mohammed V, opposite Cyberpark; admission free; ⏰ 9.30am-12.30pm & 3-7pm Mon-Sat; ♿ ⬆

Answers to your every 'how'd they make that?' are on display at this state-run artisans complex. Ringing the courtyard are set-price boutiques that give you a benchmark for the maximum you should pay for handmade brass tea trays and felt beanies in the souqs, and to the right are bigger workshops where you can watch carpets, baskets and handbags being made.

## � GALERIE NOIR SUR BLANC

☎ 024 422416; 48 Rue de Yougoslavie; ⏰ 3-7pm Mon-Fri, 10am-1pm & 3-7pm Sat

Get in on the ground floor of the Moroccan contemporary art boom at this 1st-floor showcase of major Moroccan talent. A recent show featured elemental calligraphic paintings by Marrakshi Larbi Cherkaoui, whose words break free of the page and seem to turn backflips on canvas. Friendly, well-informed staff provide useful insights about recurring motifs and fresh ideas in Moroccan art.

## � GALERIE PHOTO 127

☎ 024 432667; 2nd fl, 127 Ave Mohammed V; ⏰ 11am-7pm Tue-Sat

Like any worthwhile Chelsea gallery, this one is up a dim, once-grand staircase and in an industrial-chic chamber with the obligatory exposed brick-and-concrete wall. Shows vary from straightforward travel photography to more interpretive works, mostly by Mediterranean artists.

## � GALERIE RÉ

☎ 024 432258; http://editmanar.free.fr; Résidence Al Andalous III, cnr Rue de la Mosquée & Rue Ibn Toummert; ⏰ 9.30am-1pm & 3-8pm Tue-Sat, 11am-6pm Sun

A slick, two-storey showplace featuring emerging Moroccan artists and Mediterranean artists with connections to Morocco. Standouts include the rough-edged minimalist paintings of M'barek Bouhchichi and molten sculptures by Marrakshi Touria Othman. The gallery doubles as a publisher, issuing gorgeous illustrated editions of Arabic poetry in French.

## � HOTEL LA MAMOUNIA

☎ 024 444409; www.mamounia.com; Ave Bab Jedid; Ⓟ ♿

Once this Moorish Art Deco hotel opened in 1923, a Mamounia sticker became a must-have for any well-travelled steamer trunk –

until its unfortunate 1986 pink and beige airport lounge redesign. But the place is currently being restored to Deco glory, and you can see how top-shelf high tea in the gardens inspired even grumpy Winston Churchill to unwind and whip out the watercolours between wars. Dress to impress the doorman, who sometimes turns men away for non-head-of-state attire (ie jeans).

### ☪ JARDIN MAJORELLE
☎ 024 301852; www.jardinmajorelle .com; admission garden Dh20, museum Dh15; ☪ 8am-7pm summer, 8am-5pm winter; ♿ ☪

Not your grandma's garden, unless your grandma was a fashion icon. Landscape painter Jacques Majorelle created this splashy lemon yellow, cobalt blue and cool green modern art retreat in 1924. Decades later Yves Saint Laurent and his partner Pierre Bergère bought it as a gift for the city of Marrakesh. The Art Deco villa is now the Museum of Islamic Arts, which houses Saint Laurent's collection of decorative arts plus Majorelle's elegant lithographs of Southern Moroccan scenery. A new café on the premises offers drinks and fresh lunches at high-fashion prices, but you can't argue with the view. See p19 for more.

### ☪ MATISSE ART GALLERY
☎ 024 448326; www.matisse-art -gallery.com; 43 Passage Ghandouri, off 61 Rue de Yougoslavie; ☪ 9.30am-12.30pm & 3.30-7.30pm Mon-Sat

Polished describes this marble-fronted gallery and the contemporary Moroccan artworks it showcases. Farid Belkahia's organically shaped henna paintings evoke Berber blessings and ancient landscape formations, and you can't miss works by Marrakesh's most famous artist, Mahi Binebine. His haloed figures in natural local pigments and beeswax are tinged with melancholy, like the imprint of a loved one who's just left the room. Vintage Orientalist works are tucked away on the mezzanine, and charming gallerists will show you a treasure trove of larger contemporary works through a trap door.

### ☪ MENARA GARDENS
Ave de la Menara; garden admission free, picnic pavilion Dh20; ☪ 5.30am-6.30pm

Local lore tells of a sultan who seduced guests over dinner, then lovingly chucked them in the Menara Gardens' reflecting pools to drown. But nowadays dunking seems the furthest thing from the minds of couples canoodling poolside amid these royal olive groves. Clear days bring families for picnics in a stately 19th-century pavilion.

Stay for sunsets against the Atlas mountain backdrop, but skip the evening sound-and-light show, a 65-minute flag-waving version of Marrakshi history featuring lasers and awkward interpretive dance.

# SHOP

### ☐ ACIMA SUPERMARKET *Food*
☎ 024 430453; 109 Ave Mohammed Abdelkrim el-Khattabi; ☉ 8.30am-11pm
When you're homesick for modern convenience, here you have it: all the picnic fixings and trekking snacks you could want, when you want them, in an air-conditioned, tidy supermarket. Offers a vast selection of foods, household goods, wine and beer.

### ☐ ACR LIBRAIRIE D'ART
*Bookshop*
☎ 024 446792; www.acr-edition.com; 55 Blvd Mohammed Zerktouni, Guéliz; ☉ 9am-1.30pm & 3.30-7.30pm Mon-Fri
Marrakesh's best selection of coffee-table (or would that be mint tea–table?) books, including handsome ones on Moroccan arts and architecture, cookbooks, and how-to guides on *tadelakt* (polished plaster), *zellij* (mosaic) and other local crafts. Most are produced by Arab-French publisher ACR Editions, but there are some locally published and English-language books too. Ask the savvy staff about upcoming art openings, and local artists who offer classes. The shop is at the end of a pedestrian passageway.

### ☐ AFRICAN LODGE
*Homewares*
☎ 024 439584; 1 Rue Loubnan
Before you hanker after camel-saddle coffee tables and henna-painted orb table lamps at this ultramod African design showcase, look into shipping at the DHL office around the corner. The ingenious chandelier made out of vintage crystals and twisted industrial wire looks like something an itsy glitzy spider might have made, and is certain to make design aficionados curse carry-on restrictions.

### ☐ ALRAZAL
*Children's & Women's Fashion*
☎ 024 437884; 55 Rue Sourya; ☉ 9.30am-1pm & 3.30-8pm Mon-Sat
No abracadabra is necessary to turn little ones into a fairy-tale prince or princess: a handmade, embroidered outfit from Alrazal should do the trick. For the price of what you'd pay for off-the-rack back home, you can get kiddie couture dresses and swashbuckling velvet pant sets – and yes, those silk tunics come in women's sizes right upstairs. Alterations and made-to-measure are also possible.

## ☐ BEN RAHAL CARPETS
*Carpets*

☎ 024 433275; 28 Rue de la Liberté;
⏰ 9.30am-1.30pm & 3.30-7pm Mon-Sat

For quality carpets without the usual rounds of mint tea, haggling and ceremonious hoopla, ditch the Medina and head for the fixed prices and easygoing attitudes of Ben Rahal. Don't be fooled by the size of the place: the small, careful selection may leave you spoiled for choice. Get informed about antique Berber rugs and realistic carpet prices here first, and avoid buyer's remorse in the souqs later.

## ☐ BINI OU BINEK *Fashion*
☎ 014 259157; 44 Rue Tarik ibn Ziad;
⏰ 9am-noon & 3.30-6.30pm Mon-Sat

Work that riad-relaxed look with breezy, comfortable local designs in groovy paisleys, upbeat orange and blue polka dots, and other splashy prints. Snap up a dress for the price of a T-shirt back home, and be the toast of cocktail hour at Kechmara around the corner. The shop is in the entryway of Hotel Toulousain.

## ☐ CHEZ MAHFOUD *Jewellery*
76 Marché Municipale; ⏰ 9am-7pm Mon-Sat, 9am-noon Sun

Tucked away behind the florists and butchers at the farmers market is this unexpected silver jewellery boutique. As at any Marrakshi jeweller, about half of Mahfoud's selection is imported, but the other half is worth a look: designs range from auspicious enamelled hands of Fatima to chic silver-inlaid wood earrings. Mahfoud doesn't bargain much, because he knows what you'd pay for that onyx cocktail ring on nearby Rue de la Liberté.

## ☐ CÔTÉ SUD *Homewares*
☎ 024 438448; 4 Rue de la Liberté;
⏰ 9am-1pm & 3.30-7.30pm Mon-Sat

The best-priced of the design shops along Rue de la Liberté, and the friendliest too. Downstairs, you'll discover hand-painted tea glasses, red glass chandeliers and tasselled table linens. Upstairs, you'll feel a powerful temptation to throw yourself into the embankments of pillows in white cotton cases gone wild with embroidered red flowers.

## ☐ COULEURS PRIMAIRES
*Art Supplies*

☎ 024 446720; 37 Passage Ghandouri, off Rue de Yougoslavie; ⏰ 9.30am-1pm & 3.30-7.30pm Mon-Sat

Why let Matisse hog all the glory for painting vacations in Morocco? Find your inspiration in the streets of Marrakesh, and your raw materials at Couleurs Primaires. If you think impasto sounds like something you'd have for dinner, you can find a teacher here too. Chat up the staff and they'll hook you up with artist studio visits and Arabic calligraphy lessons.

### 🏠 CRÉAZEN *Fashion*
☎ 024 432233; 32 Galerie de la Liberté, off Rue de la Liberté; 🕑 10am-1.30pm & 3.30-7.30pm Mon-Sat

CréaZen's got your back stylishly covered with modern linen tunics with geometric embroidery and *djellaba*-inspired hooded silk shirts. Snap up pants and kaftans off the rack or made to order in linen, silky combed cotton or 'Moroccan cashmere' (cotton fleece), and don't miss reasonably priced designer accessories: jewel-toned silk necklaces, sassy tasselled belts and lucky leather slippers embossed with a hand of Fatima.

### 🏠 INTENSITÉ NOMADE *Fashion*
☎ 024 431333; 139 Ave Mohammed V; 🕑 9am-1.30pm & 4-8pm Mon-Sat

Mostly couture kaftans and tunics, with prices to match – but

Looking sharp in the Nouvelle Ville

while you won't find bargains in the basement, you will find cleverly tailored men's linen shirts by major Italian and Moroccan designers that will have the folks back home wondering about your tagine-diet secrets. Hassan Hajjaj's silk-screened Pop Art T-shirt features colourful tea glasses for a Moroccan twist on Warhol, and a minutely pin-tucked ivory silk shirt duly humbles those of us who struggle with mending socks.

### 🏠 LA ROSE *Fashion*
☎ 024 420132; 70 Rue de la Liberté; ⏰ 9.30am-12.30pm & 3-8pm Mon-Sat
Designer fashion with a bonus: any of the styles you find on the rack can be modified to suit you. Prefer that hooded top in linen, or that dress with short sleeves? Consider it done. Better still, prices here are lower than you'd expect on this boutique street, and far less than chain-store retail back home.

### 🏠 LES PARFUMS DU SOLEIL *Perfume*
☎ 024 422627; www.lesparfumsdu soleil.com; Rue Tarik ibn Ziad; ⏰ 10am-1pm & 3.30-7.30pm Mon-Sat
Those tantalising Marrakshi garden scents have been blended and bottled by ethnobotanist Abderrazzak Benchaabane, whose fragrances are drawn from native flora and inspired by Berber aro-matherapy principles. 'Soir de Mar-rakesh' is a sultry stroll through a night-blooming garden, while 'Mogador' brings a coastal breeze with traces of argan oil, Kaffir lime and cedar. 'Festival' is pure head-turning, red-carpet glamour, and no wonder: Benchaabane created it in honour of the Marrakesh International Film Festival.

### 🏠 LIBRAIRIE CHATR *Bookshop*
☎ 024 447997; 19-21 Ave Mohammed V, Guéliz; ⏰ 8.30am-1pm & 3-8pm Mon-Fri, 8.30am-1pm & 4-8pm Sat
Where else can you learn about the medicinal plants of Mo-rocco while waiting in line to buy postcards, office supplies and evocative little etchings of Medina doors? A reliable source for poolside paperbacks and Somerset Maugham classics in English, hiking maps, French and Berber language dictionaries, kids' picture books and inexpensive cookery books.

### 🏠 LINÉAIRE B COSMETICS *Beauty Products*
☎ 024 433469; www.lineaire-b.com; 13 Rue Moulay Ali; ⏰ 10am-1.30pm & 3.30-7pm Mon-Sat
Flowery descriptions in French effusively promise therapeutic effects from organic local ingre-dients and superconcentrated essential oils here. Basics such as

*savon noir* (black soap) cost three times what they might in the Rahba Qedima, but the speciality items are worth the premium: rich argan oil balm scented with jasmine, after-sun lotion with Barbary figs and healing herbs, facial masks with white mud from Fez and geranium-flower essence.

### ☐ L'ORIENTALISTE
*Homewares*
☎ 024 434074; 11 & 15 Rue de la Liberté; ⊕ 10am-1.30pm & 3.30-7pm Mon-Sat

The eternal European fascination with the other side of the Mediterranean is encouraged by this boutique, packed to overflowing with enough Arabesque accessories to equip your own harem: a Deco-decadent tea service, vintage lithographs, chip-carved ebony frames and L'Orientaliste's signature fragrances in amber, jasmine and mimosa.

### ☐ MARCHÉ MUNICIPALE *Food*
Rue ibn Toumert, off Ave des Nations Unies; ⊕ 8am-7pm

This pleasant, tidy covered market does a brisk trade in all the Marrakesh essentials: preserved lemons, spices, cooking tagines and, oddly enough, tennis wear. The butchers have been relegated to the south end of the market, so you don't have to contemplate horse meat when you're in the market for roses and designer knock-off T-shirts with nonsensical slogans such as 'Dior is my home'.

### ☐ MYSHA & NITO *Fashion*
☎ 024 421638; www.mysha-nito.com; cnr Rue Tarik ibn Ziad & Rue Sourya; ⊕ 9.30am-12.30pm & 3-8pm Mon-Sat

Upstart designers bring dazzle to a quiet corner with this new red and gold boutique. The dresses for women are a tad glitzy for anyone not attending a royal wedding, but the men's deep orange and red striped tunics are destined to wow first dates. When the flirtation turns serious, Mysha & Nito's stunning gold hand-in-hand of Fatima necklace makes a princely present.

### ☐ NEWSTAND MARCHÉ MUNICIPALE *News & Magazines*
26 Marché Municipale; ⊕ 9am-7pm Mon-Sat, 9am-noon Sun

News junkies can get their fix of major English-language newspapers only a day behind, and fashionistas can take Moroccan décor ideas home with armloads of design magazines.

### ☐ SIDI GHANEM
*Factory Outlets*
Rte de Safi; ⊕ 9am-6pm Mon-Sat

The industrial quarter 4km outside Marrakesh along the Route de Safi is chock full of made-for-export design studios selling direct from their outlets. For an adventure in modern Moroccan design, hire a taxi for a couple of hours in the morning or late afternoon and troll the lanes to see what's open (hours are erratic). Score a map of the quarter at any big studio, and follow your design bliss: head to Mia Zia for Moroccan-inspired knitwear, Akkal for ceramics with striking silhouettes and unexpected colours, and Talamanzou for handwoven Berber carpets in spare modern designs.

## 📷 TESORUCCIO
*Children's Shoes*

☎ 024 422777; 28 Galerie de la Liberté, cnr Rue de la Liberté; 🕑 9.30am-12.30pm & 3.30-7.30pm Mon-Fri

If your tiny go-getter needs some traction, try these cool German-designed, Moroccan-produced, orthopaedically correct kids' shoes. Little glam rockers will go for the soft, distressed-leather combat boots, and you'll wish they had those embossed lime-green leather sneakers in your size. Kids already bored of shopping will enjoy the playground out the front (see p60).

## 📷 YAHYA *Lighting*

☎ 024 422776; www.yahyacreation.com; 61 Rue de Yougoslavie, No 49

Passage Ghandouri, Guéliz; 🕑 9.30am-1pm & 3.30-7.30pm Mon-Thu & Sat, 9.30am-1pm Fri

These fabulous filigree lamps take the play of light to the next level: flip the switch and beams of light wink and flirt all around the room. Pity those geometric chandeliers aren't more portable, but the lozenge-shaped wall sconces and egg-shaped table lanterns add instant intrigue to dark corners. Shipping can be arranged, but insurance from Morocco isn't yet available from most shipping services – better to buy a bag and carry it on.

## 🍴 EAT

### 🍴 AL FASSIA
*Moroccan Á La Carte*                    $$

☎ 024 434060; www.bledalfassia.com; 55 Blvd Mohammed Zerktouni, 1st fl, Guéliz; 🕑 noon-10.30pm Wed-Sun

Thank goodness Al Fassia is á la carte, if only to save gourmets from our own gluttony. The array of nine starters alone is a proper feast, with orange-flower water and wild herbs raising even the lowly carrot to a crowning achievement. But there's no resisting the legendary mains, cooked Middle Atlas style by an all-women team who present the dishes with a heartfelt *b'saha* (to your health). The generous helpings seem impossible to finish, but look around and you'll see glassy-eyed diners valiantly gripping morsels of bread, scraping the last savoury caramelised onion from what was once a Berber pumpkin and lamb tagine. The seasonal menu offers enough delights for two lifetimes, but dauntless diners can call ahead to order slow-cooked lamb shoulder for two, which takes a day to prepare – and to get good and hungry.

### 🍴 ALIZIA *Mediterranean* $$
☎ 024 438360; Rue Echouhada, cnr Ave Chawki; ⏰ 7pm-midnight
Al fresco dining that's sort of French, sort of Italian, and quintessentially Marrakshi. Good food and even better people-watching: in one corner of the garden, local internet daters attempt to impress one another, while in another chic Moroccan girlfriends out of a long-lost Marrakesh episode of *Sex in the City* dish over dinner and drinks.

### 🍴 AMANDINE *Patisserie* $
☎ 024 449612; 177 Rue Mohammed el-Beqal; ⏰ 6am-11pm; ♿
Upstanding Viennoiserie without the dreary weather and with less angsty company: Amandine is every Northern European expat's dream come true. Observe local internet daters lingering over their coffee or knocking it back in

record time at the marble-topped espresso bar, then pop over to the sunny dessert salon for deceptively light chocolate mousse cake studded with raspberries.

### 🍴 BEYROUTH *Lebanese* $$
☎ 024 423525; 9 Rue Loubnan
The best possible Lebanese response to Morocco's claim to have the supreme southern Mediterranean cuisine is the smoky, silky baba ghanoush at Beyrouth – one bite and you'll want to take some to a hammam and bathe in it. Bright, lemony, Lebanese flavours are the latest foodie trend to hit Marrakesh, and this intimate restaurant serves up the best in town at reasonable prices: a mix-and-match *mezze* (starters) for two offers enough tabbouleh, spinach pies and felafel to be a meal in itself for Dh160.

### 🍴 CAFÉ 16 *Patisserie* $
☎ 024 339670; 18 Place du 16 Novembre; ⏰ 9am-midnight
The ultramod, citrus-and-blond-wood décor may seem oddly Dubai, but this double-height storefront of delights is an overnight sensation in the otherwise awkward, vast brick plaza of Place du Novembre 16. Coffee, tea and lunch options are respectable, but what crowds of fashionable Marrakshis queue for are fantasy versions of cake and ice cream:

### Saïda Chab

*Co-owner with her sisters of Al Fassia (p47), the legendary Marrakesh restaurant started by her mother*

**Favourite ingredient** Honestly? Onions. They're the most lowly, overlooked vegetable, but they add such richness and that velvety texture when you cook them well. **Must-have Marrakshi dishes** Try out different versions of Moroccan salads and tagines with seasonal vegetables – at the restaurant, our Berber farm tagine gets its savouriness from milk added at the last minute to wake up the spices. **Holiday treat** For Aïd al-Fitr (p164), I love *boulfef* (Moroccan tripe) – it's hard to make, but it's not a holiday without tripe, right? [laughs] **Chab family cooking secret revealed** Always buy your own ingredients from the producer; industrially raised chicken can't compare, it doesn't have the same flavour. Go straight to the source, even if it takes longer, and you'll taste the difference. My mother left home at 4.30am to get the very best vegetables for the restaurant, and for her it wasn't a hardship – it was a satisfaction.

NEIGHBOURHOODS

NOUVELLE VILLE

deliriously light multilayered raspberry mousse cake, or velvety chocolate coffee cream cake topped with gold leaf, and ice creams in such palate-waking flavours as lavender or basil and lemon.

### CATANZARO *Italian* $$
☎ 024 433731; 11 Rue Tarik ibn Ziad; ⏰ noon-2.30pm & 7.30-11pm Mon-Sat;  V

Where are we, exactly? The thin-crust, wood-fired pizza says Italy, the wooden balcony and powerful air-con suggest the Alps, but the spicy condiments and spicier clientele are definitely midtown Marrakesh. Grilled meat dishes are juicy and generous, but the breakout star of the menu is the Neapolitan pizza loaded with capers, local olives and Atlantic anchovies.

### KECHMARA *Continental* $
☎ 024 422532; www.kechmara.com; 3 Rue de la Liberté, Guéliz; ⏰ noon-11pm; V

If you can tear yourself away from the white and chrome décor, eye-candy waitstaff, and fashionable locals discussing affairs in Saarinen chairs, you might find the menu of interest. Respectable sandwiches and salads can be had for under Dh100, not to mention there's excellent cappuccino and aperitifs upstairs on the roof terrace.

### LA TABLE DU MARCHÉ
*French* $$$
☎ 024 424100; www.christophe-leroy.com; 4 Rue de Temple, Hivernage

Chef Christophe Leroy remakes his St Tropez market menu Marrakesh-style, juicy and decadent: succulent filet mignon crowned with a slab of seared foie gras and Coquille St Jacques slipping into a silky pear fondue. The outdoor villa setting is convivial, the plush seats comfy and the music groovy –

**As good as they look: treats at Café 16 (p48)**

Espresso with style at Kechmara

too bad the computerised music mix was interrupted with a bleep every time an instant message arrived. But when the surprisingly modest cheque arrives, you'll be quite pleased with your bleeping great meal.

### 🍴 LE CHAT QUI RIT *Italian*  $

☎ 024 434311; 92 Rue de Yougoslavie

Plenty of other places in Marrakesh serve pasta, but this place does it best: al dente, tossed with fresh produce and herbs, and drizzled with fruity olive oil. Seasonal seafood options are also a good bet, with fixings just in from the coast daily. Happy locals throng the rustic, relentlessly cheerful dining room and patio, with the namesake 'laughing cat' stencilled on sunny yellow walls, and Corsican chef/owner Bernard comes out to ask about everyone's pasta with a gleam in his eye: he already knows the answer.

### 🍴 LE GRAND CAFÉ DE LA POSTE *Mediterranean*  $$

☎ 024 433038; www.grandcafedela poste.com; Blvd el-Mansour Eddahbi, cnr Ave Imam Malik; ⏲ 8am-1am

Once a French colonial hotel and favourite café of the dread Pasha Glaoui, this place has recently been restored to its flapper-era, potted-palm glory – minus the despots, plus two inventive chefs and the odd celebrity (hello Tom Hanks and Lawrence Fishburne). Mediterranean chef Cyril Lignac is joined in the kitchen by Moroccan Sana Gamas to create a seamless blend of cuisines in signature dishes: roast chicken with wild Berber thyme and olives, grilled local sardines with tomato marmalade, and a stellar salad with local goat cheese and citrus-herb vinaigrette that will have you smacking your lips for days after.

### 🍴 LOLO QUOI *Italian*  $$

☎ 024 439757; 82 Ave Hassan II; ⏲ 7.30am-midnight Mon-Sat; 🍴

Mind the tomatoes and candles artfully strewn along the entry-way, and step into a deep-red inner sanctum with gilded poetry shimmering on the walls and mood lighting in tin buckets. Of all the restaurants where you're pay-ing for the ambience in Marrakesh, Lolo Quoi delivers – but the food

holds up its end of the bargain too. Now under the same owner-ship as Le Grand Café de la Poste, this place is jumping with a new alcohol license and a more daring seasonal menu with liberal use of terrific local goat cheese – and the tiramisu is as tasty as ever.

### 🍴 NIAGARA *Italian*  $

☎ 024 449775; 31 Centre en-Nakhil, Rte de Targa; ⏲ noon-2.15pm & 7.15-11pm Tue-Sun

When Catanzaro is packed to the rafters, do what the locals do: head to the north end of town for wood-fired pizzas at an even better price than Catanzaro. Mar-rakshi families crowd in during the day and early evening, and hipsters flock like homing pigeons to the covered roof terrace as the evening wears on – reservations are a good idea here too.

### 🍴 OLIVERI
*Ice-cream Parlour*  $

☎ 024 448913; 9 Blvd el-Mansour Eddahbi; ⏲ 9am-10pm; 🍴 🍴

Thermometers aren't necessary in Marrakesh; all you need to gauge the heat are the lines at Oliveri. Ice creams have been made on these premises for 50 years, and while the seasonal fresh fruit varieties are admirable, it's the pistachio that will inspire you to get in line all over again.

## 🍴 PÂTISSERIE ADAMO
*Patisserie*　　　　　$

☎ 024 439419; www.traiteur-adamo
.com; 44 Rue Tariq ibn Ziad; 🕙 7am-7pm
Chocolate éclairs with élan and light custard pastries studded with berries: is that rumbling your stomach, or the sound of Parisian patisseries' thunder being stolen by this Marrakshi success? Thank the seven saints of Marrakesh that chef Bruno Maulion saw fit to leave his Paris patisserie business, relocate to Marrakesh and raise the Marrakshi bar for croissants to the heavens.

## 🍴 PÂTISSERIE AL-JAWDA
*Moroccan Patisserie*　　$

☎ 024 433897; www.al-jawda.com;
11 Rue de la Liberté; 🕙 8am-7.30pm;
🚲 Ⓥ 🚼
Care for a sweet, or perhaps 200 different ones? Hakima Alami can set you up with sweet and savoury delicacies featuring figs, orange-flower water, desert honey and other local, seasonal ingredients. Around the corner at 84 Ave Mohammed V, Hakima's savvy son has set up a tea salon featuring his mother's treats plus additional savoury items such as *briouats* (stuffed pastry 'cigars') and *khlii*, the seasoned dried Berber beef that's a very acquired taste.

## 🍴 PLATS HAJ BOUJEMAA
*Marrakesh Specialities*　　$

25 Rue ibn Aicha; 🕙 noon-8pm Tue-Sun
While daredevil carnivores gnaw on dubious Djemaa grills atop rickety stools, local foodie connoisseurs calmly enjoy their scrumptious sheep's brain under sidewalk umbrellas at Haj Boujemaa. Check out the fresh meat at the refrigerated counter, and just point at whatever parts strike your fancy – you can trust the Haj to cook it to perfection. Even when properly cooked until golden, the sheep's testicles have a floury texture that's hard to get over, not to mention stringy bits that stick in your teeth, but the chips are fantastic.

## 🍴 SAMAK AL BAHRIA
*Seafood*　　　$

Blvd Moulay Rachid, cnr Rue Mauritanie;
🕙 noon-10pm Tue-Sun
Another local secret hiding in plain sight, this cheerful sidewalk joint serves top-notch Moroccan-style fresh fish and chips, with perfectly tender fried calamari just in from the coast, generous chunks of lemon, and salt and cumin to season. The sign is in Arabic, but you're in the right place when there's another fish restaurant next door, a swanky café at the corner and a mural of happy fish unaware of their dining destiny over the counter.

NEIGHBOURHOODS

NOUVELLE VILLE

# DRINK

## AFRIC'N CHIC *Bar*

☎ 024 431424; www.africnchic.com; 6
Rue Oum Errabia; ⏱ 7pm Mon-Sat
This easygoing 'Afro-Brazilian Moroccan' hot spot run by a Brazilian-French couple draws local crowds for the Monday to Friday buy one, get one free happy hour from 7pm to 9pm. By the time the live samba and bossa nova kicks in, you'll be feeling the vibe, if not buying the odd tapas menu featuring such 'Afro-Brazilian Moroccan' standbys as baked Camembert, salmon tartare and Thai salad. Say what? Stick with the fun international crowd and Moroccan mint caipirinhas at the bar, and drink those borders away.

## BAR DU SOLEIL *Bar*

☎ 024 444409; www.mamounia.com;
Hotel la Mamounia, Ave Bab Jedid;
⏱ cocktails 7-9pm; &
Wild raves for the Mamounia's gardens are a credit to its legions of gardeners but also the bartender at Bar du Soleil, who pours drinks extra strong on the patio at sunset to set that idyllic Mamounia mood. This occasion calls for a cognac or a top-shelf Mamounia cocktail of Grand Marnier, rum, juice and champagne, which, at Dh240, gives a double meaning to the term stiff drink.

## CAFÉ DES NÉGOCIANTS
*Café*

☎ 024 435782; Place Abdel Moumen
Ben Ali, cnr Ave Mohammed V & Blvd Mohammed Zerktouni; ⏱ 6am-11pm; & ♿
Cafés are usually the domain of older men in Morocco, but hipsters and headscarf-clad moms mingle with the old-timers here. The regulars have seen it all before: royalty, rebel rockers, supermodels, grandmothers and after 10pm a certain type of *négociant* (businessman) in clingy Dolce & Gabbana working the Café Atlas across the street. Enjoy the show for the Dh10 price of a truly eye-opening coffee; no alcohol.

## CAFÉ DU LIVRE *Café*

☎ 024 432149; www.cafedulivre.com;
44 Rue Tariq ibn Ziad; ⏱ 9.30am-9pm
Mon-Sat
Where the literati of Marrakesh meet and flirt shamelessly over heated poetry discussions and killer chocolate cake. Join in the fray or casually eavesdrop (everyone does) as you tuck into a salad or take advantage of the wi-fi. Wall-to-wall bookshelves of new and used titles will never leave you wanting for riad reading material, and be sure to check the door downstairs for announcements of readings and other fabulous arty events.

## ☝ LA CASA Bar

☎ 024 448226; www.elandalous-marra kech.com; Hôtel el-Andalous, Ave President Kennedy, Hivernage; admission free; ☽ 7.30pm-2am

Where else will you witness restaurant patrons delivering such heart-rending, quasi-English renditions of an Usher R&B ballad, followed by double-jointed hip shake to Jamaican dancehall and Egyptopop? Two-for-one specials on Red Bull and vodka from 7pm to 10pm get the dancing started before dinner ends, and give the neon Berber glyphs on the wall a hallucinatory glow.

## ☝ LAWRENCE BAR Bar

☎ 024 425600; www.sofitel.com; Rue Harroun Errachid, Hivernage; admission & tapas free with drink; ☽ 6.30pm-2am; ✇

One of the two bars in the sprawling 350-room Sofitel, this one advertises 'exclusive drinks' – meaning, what, your cocktail may be refused entry to your gullet if it's not properly attired? In reality this place is a freeloader's paradise, with access to a decent tapas buffet with a drink, and free bubbly if you cosy up to that diplomat splashing out the Dom Perignon rosé and don't mind the Cuban cigar smoke.

## ☝ LE COMPTOIR Bar

☎ 024 437702; www.comptoir darna.com; Rue Echouhada, Hivernage; admission free with drink or dinner; ☽ 8pm-1am; ✇

More international advances are made within the candlelit red walls of this decadent Art Deco villa than in the receiving room of the royal palace down the street. Besotted Swiss bankers lock eyes with Rabati socialites over tapas, and Italian fashionistas bat eyelashes at Moroccan musicians and French rapper MC Solar while pretending to check out the merch at the Comptoir boutique. When conversation gets too intriguing to be interrupted by squadrons of shimmying belly dancers at regular intervals, head out to the cushion-strewn courtyard. Le Comptoir is located near Hotel Imperial Borj.

## ☝ SOUKARA Bar

☎ 024 431885; www.soukara.com; cnr Ave Mohammed VI & Ave Mohammed Abdelkrim el-Khattabi; ☽ 9pm-1am

To kill time in style while waiting for a performance at the nearby Théâtre Royal – or train or Supratour bus around the corner – enjoy mint tea on the patio or a little something stiffer on the terrace. The combination of trendy Moroccan Zen décor and better prices than most Nouvelle Ville

**NEIGHBOURHOODS**

**NOUVELLE VILLE**

bars lures in the young Marrakshi set, who slyly check each other out at afternoon meetings of thinly disguised 'study groups' and make their moves over happy hour.

# PLAY

## ACTOR'S *Club*

☎ 024 339999; Hotel Atlas Medina & Spa, cnr Ave Mohammed VI & Rue Moulay el-Hassan; admission Dh150; ☽ midnight-4am

Black, white, and always ready to make a scene, Actor's was recently launched at the Marrakesh International Film Festival to give crowds a place to bask in reflected red-carpet glory. The wall-sized black-and-white photos of pale models with enormous sunglasses, Sofia Loren hats and red lipstick set a kitschy '80s vibe. During the week you might be the only one to appreciate clever DJ dance remixes, but on weekends clubbers descend from Casablanca to revive the last days of disco.

## BÔ ZIN *Club*

☎ 024 388012; www.bo-zin.com; Douar Lahna, km3.5 Rte de l'Ourika; admission free with drink; ☽ 8pm-1am; ☒ Ostensibly a restaurant with Thai touches, Bô Zin's real appeal is eye candy, Asian-Moroccan architectural razzle-dazzle, and break-out performances by din-

ers including the likes of Salma Hayek. Go late and on weekends, when it's packed; otherwise, this enormous place is a party desperately waiting to happen. It's a haul from town, so you might want to take up the offer of a chauffeur (available on request) or go with a group by taxi. It's not that far from Pacha Marrakesh (p59) if you really want to make a night/morning of it.

## CANAL FORME *Gym*

☎ 024 339580; www.marrakechcanal forme.com; 53 Ave Abou Bakker Essadik; ☽ 8am-9pm Mon-Fri, 9am-7pm Sat, 9am-1pm Sun

Trips through the souqs are enough of a workout under normal circumstances – but when a Marrakshi invites you for a 'simple meal' at which you will inevitably be urged to eat twice your weight in roast lamb, a trip to the gym might not be such a bad idea. In addition to the gym equipment, this six-floor(!) spa and fitness centre offers squash courts, African dance classes and an indoor pool with underwater spinning classes. Prices vary depending on your choice of activity.

## CINÉMA COLISÉE *Cinema*

☎ 024 448893; Blvd Mohammed Zerktouni, near Rue Mohammed el-Beqal; tickets Dh25-35; ☽ shows at 3pm, 7pm & 9.30pm

Most of the Marrakesh International Film Festival events are held at this plush cinema, so that might be David Lynch's seat you're sitting in – no wonder the evening seems a little surreal. Women come here frequently, without being asked if they come here often.

### 🌟 DIAMANT NOIR *Club*
☎ 024 434351; Hotel Marrakesh, cnr Mohammed V & Rue Oum Errbia; admission from Dh100; ⏰ 10pm-4am

For its rare gay-friendly clientele on weeknights and seedy charm on weekends, the gravitational pull of 'Le Dia' is undeniable. The dark dance floor thumps with hip hop and gleams with mirrors and bronzer on exposed skin, while closeted Casablanca playboys hold court at the tables and professionals lurk at the shady end of the upstairs bar. Cash only.

### 🌟 GENERATION QUAD
*Bicycle Hire*
☎ 067 952875; Place de la Liberté; rental per day Dh70; ⏰ 10am-1pm & 3-7pm

Bicycles can be rented at this conveniently located spot in the centre of Nouvelle Ville – and once you've successfully navigated your first roundabout the rest of your two-wheeled adventure should be as simple as riding a bike. There

are no bike lanes in Marrakesh, so requesting and wearing a helmet even in the heat is highly advisable. No matter how much of it you lose while cycling, water can be replenished; the same cannot be said for your skull.

### 🌟 INSTITUT FRANÇAIS
*Theatre/Cinema*
☎ 024 446930; www.ifm.ma; Rte de Targa, near Ave Mohammed V

Since the Théâtre Royal's indoor theatre is still under construction, this is the main year-round venue for concerts by international musicians, performances by travelling dance troupes and independent Moroccan cinema. Flyers with programme listings can be found at most Marrakshi cultural institutions, including Dar Chérifa (p98).

### 🌟 JAD MAHAL *Club*
☎ 024 436984; 10 Rue Haroun Errachid, Hivernage; admission free with drink/dinner

Through the restaurant at the far end of the courtyard, the Jad Mahal's bar is a favourite local spot to linger over cocktails by the bronze elephant until staff crank up the volume on a catchy song, the house cover band arrives, or diners break into spontaneous dance moves over an '80s tune, whichever comes first.

## JARDIN HARTI *Park*

**Rue Ouadi el-Makhazine, near Central Post Office;** 8am-7pm;
Where the action is for sporty types, active kids and amateur botanists. As well as the soccer fields, there's a playground and an outdoor amphitheatre where free shows are held. The amphitheatre doubles as an after-school hangout; and there's recently restored paths through gardens of cacti and rare succulents that will test your ability to discern euphorbia from echinocactus.

## KAWKAB JEUX
*Children's Play Centre*

024 438229; www.kawkab-jeux.com; **1 Rue Imame Chafaï, near Royal Tennis Club; admission varies;** 3-11.30pm Mon-Fri, 9.30am-midnight Sat & Sun
When your kid wearily protests at yet another carpet store, it's time for a rejuvenating visit to Kawkab Jeux. For Dh100 to Dh200 depending on the activity, you can let Junior loose on arts and crafts projects led by Kawkab's chipper staff, and buy yourself time to haggle at your leisure. Kids may have to be pried away from the mini-train, playground slides, video games, foosball table and snack bar.

## LE PARADISE *Club*

024 339100; www.leparadiseclub.com; **Hotel Mansour Eddahbi, Ave Mohammed VI;** 8pm-2am
The dance floor here doubles as a runway for Marrakesh's jet set, and it's taken such a relentless pounding over the years that it recently had to be redone. Now the redesigned two-storey club has a snazzy new look, some trippy new light effects, and a 1st-floor bar called Le Before where you can summon some liquid courage before entering the fray.

## LE THÉÂTRO *Club*

024 448811; **Hôtel es-Saadi, Ave Qadissia, Hivernage;** 11pm-4am

---

### GO KAWKABI BOO, TUNISIA!

Football fan behaviour in Morocco is generally more genteel than, ahem, England, though it always helps if you're cheering for the same team as the people sitting next to you. Usually this team is Morocco's own Lions of the Atlas, who often make it to the World Cup finals – otherwise, it's any team but Tunisia, Morocco's archrival on the field. Local teams to watch include Marrakesh's stellar Kawkab, Raja Casablanca, MAS Fez and Rabat's Fath. Support the home team and maybe your fellow fans will explain all those shouts at the referee. It's probably *'Seer al muk!'*, a shaming idiom loosely translatable as 'How can you face your mother?'.

Before you even enter Le Théâtro, you'll feel its pulsating bass line tickle your toes. Don't bother schmoozing the bouncer for entry to the boring VIP area, because the dance floor is where the action is: packed, sweaty, carefree, fabulous. White nights do happen this close to the equator on Saturdays, when the crowd wears white and keeps going 'til dawn with a signature mix of house, techno, R&B and Moroc-pop.

### ⬛ LES SECRETS DE MARRAKESH Hammam

☎ 024 434848; 62 Rue de la Liberté, Guéliz; ⏱ 10am-8pm Mon-Sat

This ultramodern hammam in an Art Deco villa is a real find. Follow the candlelit orange niches along the graphite *tadelakt* walls to the inner sanctum, the all-black hammam. House specialities include the Atlas cedar *gommage* scrub with ginger and woodsy essential oils (Dh280), a desert sand and essential oil exfoliation (Dh 250), and the full treatment with hammam, massage, Essaouira salt scrub and the ultimate carpet-shop detox: a mint tea wrap (Dh580).

### ⬛ MAMOUNIA CASINO Casino

☎ 024 444409; www.mamounia.com; Hotel la Mamounia, Ave Bab Jedid; ⏱ slots from 4pm, gaming tables from 8pm; ♿

As if drinking OJ from re-used glasses in Djemaa el-Fna weren't enough of a gamble, just down the street is Mamounia Casino. There are many places in Marrakesh that look like a Vegas version of Morocco, but the casino makes good on the comparison with blackjack, poker, baccarat, roulette and slot machines. Dress to pass the doorman – sorry, even high rollers don't get by in jeans.

### ⬛ PACHA MARRAKESH Club

☎ 024 388405; www.pachamarrakech.com; Zone Hôteliére, Blvd Mohammed VI; Mon-Wed admission free, Thu Dh100, Fri & Sat Dh200; ⏱ 8pm-5am, pool access noon-7pm; ⛶ ♿

Pacha Ibiza was the prototype for this enormous disco, but Marrakesh has smashed that mould with its own international DJ line-up playing to huge weekend influxes of Casablanca hipsters and raging Rabatis. The complex includes two restaurants, the very cool Chill-Out lounge bar, and a pool where you can lounge in the afternoon (day entry Dh150) until the party starts – but they've got you where they want you to charge major dirhams for drinks, so savvy clubsters smuggle in water. Pacha doesn't come close to hitting its 3000 occupancy during the week, and it's a long way to come to drink alone, so bring your own entourage.

### ☆ ROYAL TENNIS CLUB
*Tennis Club*

☎ 024 431902; www.frmtennis.com; Jardin Harti, Rue Ouadi el-Makhazine; per hr Dh100; ☼ 7am-noon & 2.30-10pm

King Hassan II loved his tennis, as witnessed by numerous portraits of the guy in all-white togs at this historic 1926 tennis venue complete with clubhouse and pool. Perfect your own royal backhand with helpful instructors on one of seven clay courts (or more, depending on your aim), including the centre court named after Moroccan tennis legend Younes el Ayanaoui. Mornings and evenings are usually best; four courts are lit at night.

### ☆ TANZANIA *Club*

☎ 024 422449; Moulay Hassan I Kawkab Center, Rue Moulay el-Hassan; admission free with dinner/drinks; ☼ 8pm-1am

Gazebos get groovy with lounge music and animal-print cushions, and there's plenty of room to bust dance moves among the palms. Fire eaters and belly dancers complete the strangest garden scene outside of a William S Burroughs novel. The pizza's tough and bland, but the drinks are well spiked.

### ☆ TESORUCCIO PLAYGROUND
*Children's Playground*

ground fl, Immeuble Liberté, cnr Ave Mohammed V & Rue de la Liberté

Here's the secret of all those chic Marrakshiyya mothers: a playground tucked inside an arcade right off Rue de la Liberté, which has some of the best shopping in town and excellent day spas for a touch of pampering. Stop in to placate shopworn kids, or leave your co-parent in charge while you cut loose.

### ☆ THÉÂTRE ROYAL *Theatre*

☎ 024 431516; 40 Blvd Mohammed VI; admission free to foyer, ticket prices vary

Tunisian architect Charles Boccara's Maghrebi monument features Egyptian Art Deco papyrus pillars, a Sahara sand-coloured portico, and showstopping Moroccan exposed brickwork in the domed foyer. Twenty-five years in the making, the Théâtre Royal is a sore subject for Marrakshis still waiting for a completed interior – apparently the work wasn't done to specifications, the money's gone, and the whole legal ordeal's become a monumental embarrassment. Meanwhile regular performances are held in a Carthage-style outdoor amphitheatre with hard seats but terrific acoustics.

### ☆ VIP *Club/Cabaret*

☎ 024 434569; Place de la Liberté, across from Hotel Marrakesh; Dh150 (incl 1 drink), free before 1am; ☼ 11pm-4am

Head through the '80s fuchsia neon entryway, and you'll find two venues for the price of one: a disco that gets the party started with high-energy techno, and a cabaret where musicians pound out raucous Rai-Gnaoua-Chaabi fusion. The crowd is gay-friendly and fashion conscious, though some bar lurkers are working more than a look.

# > PALMERAIE

This 5260-hectare oasis 5km east of the Medina once had as many as 150,000 palm trees, but that number is dwindling fast as prime Palmeraie real estate gets snapped up for lavish hotels and private villas. To see a natural oasis, come quick – there may soon be more celebrities than trees here, unless the local nonprofit tree-planting programme takes root (to help, see p157). Dromedary safaris through the palms provide prime photo ops, and cycling (bikes are available in downtown Marrakesh and from Jnane Tamsna, p133) and horseback riding are idyllic ways to take in the oasis scenery without harming its delicate ecosystem (as quads and dune buggies do). Amid the palms you might discover new talents, with cooking classes or English-language arts and crafts courses on offer. Also worth the trip from downtown Marrakesh are outstanding hammams and lounging opportunities at some of the plusher Palmeraie villa guest-houses – if you'd like to stay here, check out p133. One thing to factor into your budget is transport to/from the Palmeraie: taxis from Marrakesh will cost upwards of Dh50, and private taxi services routinely charge as much as Dh150 to Dh200 for pick up/drop off to Palmeraie nightspots.

# PALMERAIE

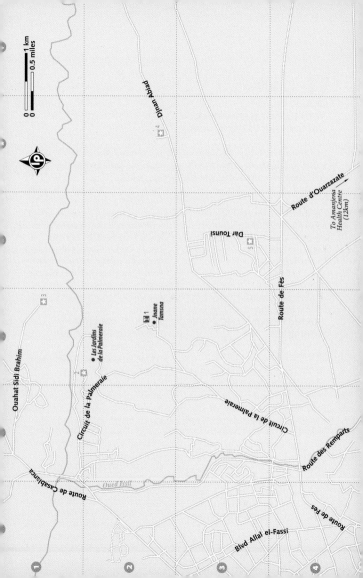

#  DRINK

## ABYSSIN *Bar*

☎ 024 328584; www.restaurant-labyssin.com; Palais Rhoul, km5 Rte de Fès, Dar Tounsi

Like Lindsay Lohan at a garden party, you and your entourage can score your own plush, private pavilion at the Palais Rhoul. To get to your seat, you'll have to strut the runway in the middle of the reflecting pool. This may prove more difficult as the evening wears on and bottles of wine and champagne are drained – but you must walk this way to reach the bathroom, which has been thoughtfully padded with white leather from floor to ceiling to accommodate stumbles and minor breakdowns.

## LES DEUX TOURS *Bar*

☎ 024 329525; www.les-deuxtours.com; Douar Abiad, Circuit de la Palmeraie

Settle into a chaise longue by the pool or a butterfly chair on the lawn, and order something fruity from the bar. Service can be slow, but what's the big hurry? Slap on some sun block, crack the binding of that novel and stay awhile. Combine your lounging session with a trip to Les Deux Tours Hammam (p66), and you may have to be peeled off your beach towel.

#  PLAY

## CLUB EQUESTRE DE LA PALMERAIE GOLF PALACE

*Horse Riding*

☎ 024 368793; www.pgp.co.ma; Les Jardins de la Palmeraie, Circuit de la Palmeraie; per hr from Dh150; ⏲ 8am-noon & 3-6pm

Dash off into the desert on your trusty steed from this stable, which conveniently offers lessons and well-behaved horses for novice riders who can't tell their bridle from their bit. Parents in desperate need of a hammam can bribe kids with a pony ride – the miniature ponies are way beyond cute, and the paddock is a safe, easy ride.

## KASBAH LE MIRAGE DROMEDARY SAFARIS

*Camel Rides*

☎ 024 314444; www.kasbahlemirage.com; Ouahat Sidi Brahim

Camels seem to lurk under every palm in the Palmeraie awaiting tourists they can lug a few blocks and then spit at, but for a longer ride on good-tempered dromedaries, Kasbah Le Mirage offers 90-minute trips (per person Dh290) – just long enough to entertain Lawrence of Arabia fantasies, but shorter than the director's cut. Just don't blame us if you discover your inner nomad and ditch your cushy Cairo desk job for more desert adventures.

**Meryanne Loum-Martin**
*Parisian lawyer turned tastemaker and sustainable-travel champion as creator of Jnane Tamsna (p133)*

**How Marrakesh differs from Dubaï** Given the great natural patrimony here, environmental impact has become an obsession. Visitors care about it too, so there's a good base for responsible tourism. **What a weekend can do** We see it all the time here: even when people come for a short break to swim or play tennis, they want to give back to the community. We encourage them to plant palms through [husband Gary Martin's] Global Diversity Foundation and support local initiatives like Dar Taliba girls' school (p157). **The well-read Red City** Café du Livre (p54) is wonderful, and at Jnane Tamsna we started a literary workshop that featured Booker Prize–winner Kirin Desai – all the proceeds went to a local literacy programme. **Favourite gifts to give/get** Organic bath products from Nectarôme (see p93) and argan oil and embroidery produced by local cooperatives.

### ⭐ KSAR CHAR-BAGH HAMMAM *Hammam*

☎ 024 329244; www.ksarcharbagh.com; Djnan Abiad, off Rte de Fès; Ⓟ

A trip to this spectacular subterranean red-marble hammam is almost eerily like rebirth. Re-entry to the world is eased with scented essential oils, liberal application of Anne Semonin products and a mood-lit lounge area. There's also a swimming pool. Treat yourself to a hammam, velvety skin scrub, *rhassoul* (mud scalp rub) and 90-minute perfumed-oil massage (Dh800) and emerge vowing to be a better person – or at least wear more sunscreen.

### ⭐ LE BOWLING *Bowling Alley*

☎ 024 301010; Palmeraie Golf Palace, Circuit de la Palmeraie; per person, 10 frames DH40; ☽ noon-10pm

When the sun is too blazingly hot to move but the little ones are too restless for the riad, try this air-conditioned, quaint six-lane bowling alley for family fun out in the Palmeraie. The kitschy retro décor offers an interesting take on American geography – the Hollywood sign overlooks the Manhattan skyline, Twin Towers and all. For grownups, billiard tables and a full bar are available.

### ⭐ LES DEUX TOURS HAMMAM *Hammam*

☎ 024 329525; www.les-deuxtours.com; Douar Abiad, Circuit de la Palmeraie; Ⓟ

The Charles Boccara–designed domed hammam that started the mad dash on Moroccan hammams is still one of the most elegant, and now it has expanded its spa menu to lavish attention on you head to foot. The traditional hammam-*gommage* (body scrub) treatment combo (per 30 minutes Dh200) can be supplemented with

## LEARN

If swaying palms leave you restless or excess lounging turns your brain to mush, consider taking a course at a Palmeraie guesthouse. Prices depend on class size and duration, and may differ for guests/nonguests. Top choices:

> Learn organic Moroccan cooking at **Jnane Tamsna** (www.jnanetamsna.com) with local, sustainably sourced ingredients.
> Have the family secrets for the signature dishes of legendary restaurant Al Fassia (p47) revealed to you at cookery courses at **Bled al-Fassia** (www.bledalfassia.com).
> Make your own Moroccan-inspired crafts in English-language courses with local *maâlems* (master craftspeople) in weaving, *tadelakt* (polished plaster), *zellij* (mosaic) and *zellij* patchwork quilting at **Riad Bledna** ( ☎ 061 182090; www.riadbledna.com).

Made in the shade: relax at Les Deux Tours

massage (per 30 minutes Dh300), a dip in the pool and a cocktail (Dh70 to Dh100).

### LES PALAIS RHOUL HAMMAM *Hammam*

☎ 024 329494; www.palais-rhoul.com; Palais Rhoul, km5 Rte de Fes, Dar Tounsi; P

A classic Moroccan hammam, with separate chambers for varying levels of heat, *zellij* and *tadelakt* walls, and sunbeams filtering through vaulted ceilings. It's oddly placed alongside a French baroque villa, amid fake Berber tents pitched in a formal garden – but don't let that deter you. The standard hammam treatment (€60) includes *gommage*, *rhassoul* with orange-flower water and massage with organic essential oils, and it really Rhouls. Treat yourself to cocktails afterwards at Abyssin (p64) and you may have to be scraped up and mailed home.

# > DJEMAA EL-FNA

The magnet of Marrakesh pulls in the crowds with street theatre, magic-potion sellers, and hot competition at the nightly grilling competition with 100 cooks. 'La Place' sees action from dawn until well after midnight, and though you may be wary of pickpockets, makeshift food stalls and unpredictable scooter, donkey and horsedrawn-carriage traffic, don't miss the world's best dinner theatre right here. Do what you must – tuck cash into your underwear, bring your own utensils, wear reflective clothing – but by all means stick around to earn foodie bragging rights and see for yourself what new act is enthralling the crowds tonight. Just off the Djemaa are more dining adventures and the entry to the souqs; dive right in and emerge hours later overawed, bearing a carpet, and in need of an espresso at one of the Djemaa's cafés. Settle in and enjoy the show.

## DJEMAA EL-FNA

### 🜨 SEE

| | | |
|---|---|---|
| Djemaa el-Fna | 1 | C3 |
| Koutoubia Minaret | 2 | A5 |
| Ramparts | 3 | B4 |

### 🍴 EAT

| | | |
|---|---|---|
| Alahbab Fast Food | 4 | B4 |
| Chez Chegrouni | 5 | D3 |
| Djemaa el-Fna Food Stalls | 6 | C3 |
| Haj Mustapha | 7 | D3 |
| Ice Legend | 8 | C4 |
| La Maison du Couscous | 9 | C4 |
| Mechoui Alley | 10 | D3 |
| Narwama | 11 | A4 |
| Pâtisserie des Princes | 12 | C5 |
| Restaurant Foucauld | 13 | A5 |

### 🍸 DRINK

| | | |
|---|---|---|
| Café Argana | 14 | C3 |
| Café du Grand Balcon | 15 | C4 |
| Les Terrasses de L'Alhambra | 16 | D3 |
| Piano Bar Les Jardins de la Koutoubia | 17 | A3 |
| Restaurant/Bar du Grand Hotel Tazi | 18 | B6 |

### ⭐ PLAY

| | | |
|---|---|---|
| Hotel Ali Bike Rental | 19 | B4 |

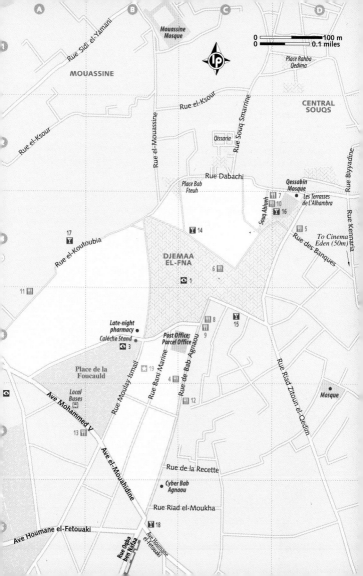

# MOUASSINE

Mouassine Mosque

Place Rahba Qedima

0 — 100 m
0 — 0.1 miles

Rue Sidi el-Yamani

Rue el-Ksour

Rue el-Ksour

Rue el-Mouassine

Rue el-Ksour

Qissaria

Rue Souq Smarrine

CENTRAL SOUQS

Rue Biyyadine

Rue Dabachi

Place Bab Fteuh

Qessabin Mosque

Souq Ablueh

Les Terrasses de L'Alhambra

10

16

5

Rue des Banques

Rue Kennaria

To Cinema Eden (50m)

17

Rue el-Koutoubia

14

DJEMAA EL-FNA

6

11

1

Late-night pharmacy

Caléche Stand

3

Post Office; Parcel Office

8

9

15

Place de la Foucauld

19

Rue Moulay Ismail

Rue Bani Marine

Rue de Bab Agnaou

Local Buses

13

Ave Mohammed V

4

12

Mosque

Rue Riad Zitoun el-Qedim

Ave el-Mouahidine

Rue de la Recette

Cyber Bab Agnaou

Rue Riad el-Moukha

Ave Houmane el-Fetouaki

18

Rue Houmane el-Fetouaki

Rue Talaa ben Nafaa

#  SEE

## DJEMAA EL-FNA

🕐 **approx 9am-1am, later during Ramadan;** ♿ 👶

Grab a front-row or balcony seat at a café alongside the Djemaa, and watch the drama unfold. As the sun travels across the sky, orange-juice vendors make way for healers and henna tattoo artists, who scoot over for snake charmers, astrologers and acrobats. Around dusk, the storytellers begin their epic tales, and cooks cart in the makings of 100 restaurants specialising in barbecued everything, tasty cooked salads and steaming snails. For the ultimate dinner theatre, look no further than the Gnaoua drummers, male belly dancers and Berber musicians surrounding the Djemaa dining action. See p10 for more.

## KOUTOUBIA MINARET

**cnr Rue el-Koutoubia & Ave Mohammed V;** 🕐 **mosque & minaret closed to non-Muslims, gardens 8am-8pm**

When the present mosque and its iconic Moorish minaret were finished by Almohad Sultan Yacoub el-Mansour in the 12th century, 100 booksellers were clustered around its base – hence the name Koutoubia, meaning 'booksellers'. In the recently refurbished gardens outside the mosque, you might still notice a recent excavation that confirmed a longstanding Marrakshi legend: the pious Almohads were apparently distressed to discover that their lax Almoravid predecessors had built a mosque that wasn't properly aligned with Mecca, and razed the place to build another. Atop the minaret are three golden balls made of copper. The originals were reputedly real gold donated by the guilt-tripping mother of a sultan after she'd sneaked a mid-day snack during Ramadan. See p16 for more.

Juice for two in the Djemaa el-Fna

## THREE MARRAKESH MUSTS FOR DARING DINERS

> Discover a back-alley taste sensation. Adventurous eaters should try Haj Mustapha (p72), Mechoui Alley (p74) or Ben Youssef Food Stall Qissaria (p86) for truly memorable meats.
> Try argan oil at Assouss Cooperative D'Argane (p99). Chefs drizzle this oil on salads and delicate dishes for a savoury, toasted-hazelnut flavour, but you won't believe how it's made. Crafty Moroccan goats clamber up argan trees to nosh on their favourite fuzzy fruit, and then pass the pits. Traditionally women collect their dung, sort out the argan pits, split them open, and press the nuts to yield this precious oil.
> Take a Moroccan cooking class: several riads offer them to guests ( p117), and La Maison Arabe (p124) offers its courses to nonguests. Jnane Tamsna (p133) teaches cooking with organic, local ingredients. Another option is **Souk Cuisine** ( ☎ 073 804955), where in three hours chef Gemma van de Burgt leads foodies through the Medina to pick out produce and spices and teaches them to whip up Moroccan specialities.

### 🎥 RAMPARTS

**calèche rides per carriage per hr Dh150**
In the 12th century, the Almoravids wrapped the Medina snugly in 19km of mud brick 5m tall, so that the city doubled as a fortress. But this didn't keep out the Almohads, who considered their predecessors irredeemably corrupt and razed the city, leaving almost no trace of their 85-year rule except for these ramparts. Today the ramparts are for lovers, not fighters, with couples patrolling the rampart gardens at sunset. Calèches are available near the Djemaa el-Fna.

### 🍴 EAT

### 🍴 AL AHBAB FAST FOOD
*Shwarma* $
☎ 071 377146; 70 Ave Prince Moulay Rachid

The awning boasting 'recommended by Lonely Planet' must be 25 years old now, and still we stand by our initial assessment of the Dh25 *shwarma* (meat sliced off a spit and stuffed in a pocket of pita-type bread with chopped tomatoes and garnish) accompanied by four sauces and just-right French fries, though the avocado milkshake is best avoided. Unlike many other fast-food joints along this strip, local women frequent this place because the chipper staff put everyone at ease. The entry is via Rue de Bab Agnaou.

### 🍴 CHEZ CHEGROUNI
*Moroccan Á La Carte* $
**northeast cnr Djemaa el-Fna, near Rue des Banques;** 🕐 8am-11pm; 🅥 👶
You'll need to grab a slip of paper from the plastic cup and write down your own order, but

the staff could probably tell at a glance anyway: you're either a gourmand searching for the classic Dh50 tagine with chicken, preserved lemons and olives; a vegetarian in for the surprisingly flavourful, vegetable-broth-only seven-vegetable couscous; or a tagine-weary traveller in dire need of a respectable omelette with superior chips. You won't be disappointed.

### 🍴 DJEMAA EL-FNA FOOD STALLS Marrakesh Specialities $
**Djemaa el-Fna;** ⏱ sunset-1am

Around sunset, donkeys descend on the Djemaa hauling gas canisters by the cartload and all the makings of 100 small restaurants. Within the hour, the restaurants are up and running, with chefs urging passers-by to note the cleanliness of their grills, the freshness of their meat, produce and cooking oil, and their aromatic spice mixes. The grilled meats and cooked salads are cheap and often tasty, and despite alarmist warnings your stomach should be fine if you use your bread instead of rinsed utensils and stick to bottled water. Adventurous foodies will want to try Marrakesh specialities such as steaming snail soup, sheep's brain and skewered hearts – always go for the busiest stalls with the freshest meats.

### 🍴 HAJ MUSTAPHA
*Marrakesh Specialities* $
**east side, Souq Ablueh (Olive Souq);** ⏱ 6-10pm

As dusk approaches, several stalls that serve *mechoui* (slow-roasted lamb) at lunchtime feature a Marrakshi speciality: paper-sealed crockpots of *tangia,* lamb traditionally slow-cooked all day in the ashes of a hammam fire. This 'bachelor's stew' is a bit messy as a takeaway order, but Haj Mustapha offers the cleanest seating despite dire bachelor décor (think faded photos in shattered picture frames). Use bread as your utensil to scoop up *tangia,* sprinkle it with fresh cumin and salt, and devour it with olives from the other side of the souq.

### 🍴 ICE LEGEND
*Ice-cream Parlour* $$
☎ 024 444200; 52 Rue de Bab Agnaou, **off Djemaa el-Fna;** ⏱ 10am-8pm

Your saving grace on scorching afternoons: fresh, locally made ice cream in modern facilities. Go with the tantalizing (if alarmingly bright) fruity varieties – the lemon sorbet here is legendary. To compensate for the male dominance of cafés, women have the run of ice-cream parlours in Morocco, so men should be prepared to surrender their seats gallantly or suffer icy stares.

### Mohamed Nour
*Geologist turned eco-savvy adventure guide for Inside Morocco Tours ( ☎ 051 182090; www.insidemoroccotours.com) and owner of Riad Bledna (p133)*

**Berber social graces** Don't be shy about visiting Berber villages around Marrakesh – they need attention and would really benefit from your visit. Accept invitations to tea, and when you do say *'b'sahaoura'* ('health and rest') and make a slurping noise when you drink – it's actually considered polite. **Tashelhit basics** *'Mament kadgheet?'* means 'How are you doing?' You can answer *'Thinna'*, 'Everything's at peace'. If you see someone in a dry place, it's polite to stop and offer water: *'Bgheetee treet aman?'* **Marrakesh myths** We still use donkeys for transport – they're very green-friendly, you know – but we've got the internet here too. **Great escapes** Everyone needs a break from Marrakesh eventually. One night away is enough to go to the Agafay Desert, the High Atlas mountains, and visit Berber villages in a hidden valley oasis. With another day, you could visit the desert kasbah – often used in movies – at Aït Benhaddou, or Pasha Glaoui's kasbah in the Telouet mountain pass. In three or four days, you could trek in Sahara dunes.

NEIGHBOURHOODS

DJEMAA EL-FNA

### 🍴 LA MAISON DU COUSCOUS
*Moroccan À La Carte*                   $

☎ 024 386892; 53 Rue de Bab Agnaou;
🕑 11.30am-10pm

With its marble fountain shaped like a conical couscous, '80s-era love of mirrors, and arctic air conditioning, this place seems like a tourist trap – but the couscous is fluffy and properly infused with fragrant *smen* (seasoned clarified butter). The Atlas chicken (no 65) is sweet-savoury with onions, and at the risk of inflaming local rivalries, the sneakily spicy Tunisian with Merguez sausage and meatballs (Dh65) is even better. The friendly staff are really into Moroccan pop, reggae and Bob Dylan, so your dinner soundtrack is more bizarrely intriguing than an MP3 player on shuffle.

### 🍴 MECHOUI ALLEY
*Marrakesh Specialities*                 $

east side, Souq Ablueh; 🕑 11am-2pm

Around lunchtime, the vendors at this row of stalls start carving up enormous steaming sides of *mechoui*, as though King Henry VIII might show up at any moment. Step right up, point to the best-looking cut of meat and ask for a *nuss* (half) or *rubb* (quarter) kilo. Some haggling might ensue, but Dh30 to Dh50 should procure you the freshest, most delicious falling-off-the-bone lamb you'll ever have.

Take two ostrich eggs and call me in the morning

With your meat comes freshly baked bread, fresh cumin, salt and some olives (though you're better off picking out your own across the way). Do not attempt to sight-see or operate heavy machinery after this narcolepsy-inducing lunch – you need naps and/or four mint teas first.

### ⚅ NARWAMA
*Moroccan–Thai*                    $$

☎ 024 442510; 30 Rue el-Koutoubia, near Djemaa el-Fna; ☿ 8pm-1am; ♿ Ⓥ

Opposites attract at Narwama, true to its name ('fire and water') with winning combinations that defy convention. It's all in the mix here: a Bangkok chef who tops tasty Thai green curries with almond-and-cream dessert *bastilla* (flaky pastry), a DJ spinning super-cool Brazilian/Italian/Arabic tunes, and the best Moroccan mint mojito in town (alcohol is served), all in a 19th-century riad with 21st-century Zen décor. Word has it the royal princesses up the street get takeaway from here.

### ⚅ PÂTISSERIE DES PRINCES
*Patisserie*                        $

☎ 024 442319; 32 Rue de Bab Agnaou, off Djemaa el-Fna; ☿ 9am-8pm; Ⓥ ♿
A sure-fire fix for blood-sugar lows, this place is beloved of kids, high-metabolism snackers and

anyone stumped for something to bring to a Moroccan dinner party. The *pain au chocolat*, at Dh2.50, is a crowd-pleaser and the assorted Moroccan petits fours (per kilo Dh130) are a very sweet thought indeed. There are better French pastries in the Nouvelle Ville, but for Moroccan sweets this one's hard to top.

### ⚅ RESTAURANT FOUCAULD
*Moroccan À La Carte*               $

☎ 024 440806; Ave el-Mouahidine, cnr Place de la Foucauld; ☿ noon-3pm & 7.30pm-midnight; Ⓥ ♿
This stucco-bedecked, dimly lit restaurant has seen many a Moroccan wedding in its day – which was at least 30 years ago, judging from copper relief landscapes from the 1970s and Bureau of Tourism posters from the French Protectorate. But this place is definitely set for a comeback with succulent lamb with figs and sesame, fresh crusty bread, and tangy harira (soup), all for Dh100.

## Ⓨ DRINK
### Ⓨ CAFÉ ARGANA *Café*
☎ 024 445350; northwest cnr, Djemaa el-Fna, near Place Bab Fteuh; ☿ 7am-11pm; ♿
One of the few cafés where you'll compete with locals for elbow room and a spectacular view of the Djemaa at sunset, when the

restaurant stalls set up shop and the belly dancers begin to wriggle. Each floor is its own distinct scene: the top balcony is a private retreat for couples and gossiping friends lingering over tea and ice cream in sweetened-cardboard flavours; the next floor down has a double balcony, with back rows for snacks and the front for passable tagines; and the ground floor is for coffee, tea and ice-cream cones.

### ▼ CAFÉ DU GRAND BALCON
*Café*

**south side, Djemaa el-Fna, near Rue Riad Zitoun el-Qedim; ⏰ 8am-10pm; ♿**
The best spot to catch all the action in the Djemaa, with permanent crowds on the front patio to prove it. Older gents hang out inside to avoid the patio jostling and panhandling on the patio, but only families and clandestine lovers actually go upstairs to the quiet 'grand balcon', where service is erratic at best. The OJ here is not freshly squeezed, but there are mean espressos, frothy cappuccinos, and proper tea with mint or steamed milk. Technically this place serves ice cream, but there's far better around the corner at Ice Legend (p72).

### ▼ LES TERRASSES DE L'ALHAMBRA *Café-Bar*
**☎ 024 427570; northeast cnr, Djemaa el-Fna; ⏰ 8am-midnight; ♿ ♿ V**

Although there's a mosque right next door, somehow this place managed to procure a liquor license – though to respect local sensibilities, enjoy your beer inside or on the upper terrace, where you can watch the storytellers pull in the crowds at sunset. By day, the tasteful Moroccan-modern décor is a sight for souq-sore eyes, and Italian Illy espresso served under terrace tent awnings will sharpen your wits for bargaining. In a pinch, the pizzas will do for carbo-loading before your next lap around the Medina.

### ▼ PIANO BAR LES JARDINS DE LA KOUTOUBIA *Bar*
**☎ 024 388800; www.lesjardinsdelakoutoubia.com; Les Jardins de la Koutoubia Hotel, 26 Rue el-Koutoubia; ⏰ 5pm-1am**
How often has the long-suffering pianist heard 'Play it again, Sam'? Probably too many to count, but he'll gamely play 'As Time Goes By', because it's that sort of classy joint. Like the fabulous hotel lobby, the décor here is all restrained Moroccan modernity, from its natural cedar ceilings to the plush Berber carpets – a fine place to unwind after your tour of duty in the souqs. Alcohol is served.

### ▼ RESTAURANT/BAR DU GRAND HOTEL TAZI *Bar*
**☎ 024 442787; Ave el-Mouahidine, cnr Rue de Bab Agnaou; ⏰ 7pm-1am**

For those who object to a Dh40 bottle of beer as a matter of proletarian principle, this place serves the cheapest in town at Dh25 to throngs of like-minded travellers and Marrakshis just off work in the souqs. The tales take a turn for the outrageous as the evening wears on, but then some of us enjoy that kind of thing.

#  PLAY

### CINÉMA EDEN *Cinema*
**Derb Dabbachi, near Rue des Banques; tickets Dh15;** ⏱ **shows at 3pm, 6pm & 9pm**
You don't know how rowdy cinema can get until you've caught a romantic comedy with the all-male audience in this mud-brick movie house tiled with broken plates, plastered with Bollywood posters and carpeted with peanuts. As Juan Goytisolo explains in *Cinema Eden: Essays from the Muslim Mediterranean*, only films with happy endings are allowed here – the management prefers evenings here to be a laugh riot, rather than any other kind.

### HOTEL ALI BIKE RENTAL
*Bicycle Hire*
☎ **024 444979; Rue Moulay Ismail**
No frills here, and no 20-speed mountain bikes either – but if the warhorse on offer still looks good after you kick the tyres and test the brakes, you'll have a whole new way to get around the Medina. As for dealing with Marrakshi traffic: ask about helmets, and consider prayer.

# > CENTRAL SOUQS & DERB DEBACHI

Souq means 'market', but when locals refer to 'the souqs' they mean the maze of market streets north of the Djemaa el-Fna and southwest of the Musée de Marrakesh. The main thoroughfare from the Djemaa el-Fna, Souq Semmarine (Leather Souq), sells a hodgepodge of local crafts, but further north the souqs are more specialised. Wander the east–west *qissarias* (covered markets) between Souqs Smata and el-Kebir (literally, 'the big souq for leatherwork') and buy direct from leather toolers, basket weavers, woodworkers and felt makers. There's another *qissaria* to the west of Koubba Ba'adiyn packed with food stalls where you can join the locals for lunch. And you'll soon discover that specialist souqs with the same names can be found elsewhere, just when you thought you knew where you were.

## CENTRAL SOUQS & DERB DEBACHI

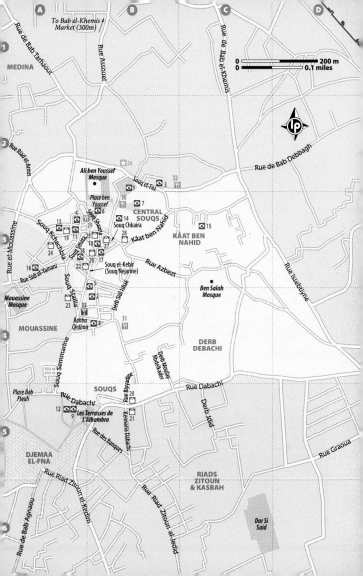

There are a few cafés at the northeast end of the souqs where you can grab a bite and catch your breath, but the action-packed central souqs are not the best place to unwind. To really experience the raucous/peaceful contrast that is the essence of Marrakesh, adjacent Derb Debachi is a calming residential area with stunning riads (see p127), and you'll find more historic riads in the Mouassine.

# SEE

## ALI BEN YOUSSEF MEDERSA
☎ 024 441893; admission Dh40, with Musée & Koubba Dh60; ⏰ 9am-6pm; ♿
This centre of Quranic learning was founded in the 14th century, and in its heyday 900 students spent all day, every day, studying religious and legal texts. A couple of the 2nd-floor 3-sq-metre dorm rooms

on the west side of the courtyard show how students lived – but they must've been a seniors' rooms, because there are many smaller ones in courtyards down the hall with sleeping lofts up makeshift ladders for a truly monastic existence. The school was updated in the 19th century, but the limited bathrooms proved a persistent problem. The medersa still exudes magnificent, studious calm – and now that tourists have the run of the place, the bathrooms are top notch. See p14 for more.

## FARNATCHIS
**Souq el-Fez, east of Ali ben Youssef Medersa**
To survive in times of siege, every Medina neighbourhood needed two things: its own fountain and a *farnatchi*, a public oven where locals brought bread to be baked. Many neighbourhoods still have

Just drink it beautiful skin guaranteed

## THE SOUQ CIRCUIT

Put your sense of direction to the ultimate test with this loop of the central souqs:

> Souq Ableuh: make like James Bond and follow the scent of 1000 martinis to the Olive Souq.
> Souq Kchacha: find your dream date in stall after stall of dried fruits in the Fruit and Nut Souq.
> Souq Semmarine: trendy handbags and handy man bags lure luggage fetishists in the Leather Souq.
> Criée Berbère (Souq Joutia Zrabi): the namesake 'Berber Call' can be heard Saturday to Tuesday around 4pm, when Atlas Mountain dealers descend for auctions in the covered Carpet Souq — but you'll be called into shops 'just for looking' anytime.
> Souq Cherratine: for centuries, equestrians have exhibited unbridled passion for the hand-tooled saddles in the Leatherworkers' Souq.
> High-Tech Souq: donkey carts haul in flat-screen TVs and computers in this anachronistic mud-brick multimedia marketplace.
> Souq Haddadine: sparks fly and hammers clang in the Blacksmiths' Souq, where old bikes become the latest lanterns; forge on to . . .
> Souq Kimakhine: musicians dawdle for days watching lutes carved and tambourines stretched in the Instrument-Makers' Souq; buy a drum and beat it to . . .
> Souq Sebbaghine: you've saved the most spectacular souq for last — the Dyers' Souq has yarn hanging from the rafters in primary colours. Wander past the bubbling vats of dye and if you're in the right Souq Sebbaghine you can head down Rue el-Mouassine back toward the Djemaa. Then it becomes official: you're a dyed-in-the-wool souq specialist.

See p12 for more.

*farnatchis,* and naturally everyone claims theirs is the best. To find a *farnatchi,* follow the smell of baking bread or anyone carrying a cloth-covered basket – or visit the one between Le Foundouk (p87) and Riad (you guessed it) Farnatchi (p128).

### ◉ HIGH-TECH SOUQ

**north of Souq Cherratine;** ⏱ **approx 9.30am-7.30pm**

Wander to the north of the souqs past the bridle-makers and lute-carvers and through a stone archway, and you'll find the most bizarre bazaar of all. This souq is covered with palm fronds and lined with shops that are literally holes in the mud-brick walls, packed floor to ceiling with flat-screen TVs. Donkey carts lug in computers still in their boxes; it's multimedia gone medieval.

## KOUBBA BA'ADIYN

**opposite Ali ben Youssef Mosque; admission Dh15, with Medersa & Koubba Dh60; 9am-7pm**

The Almohads sought to erase all trace of their Almoravid predecessors, but they mysteriously spared this small, graceful 12th-century cupola for ablutions. This is your crib sheet for Hispano-Moresque architecture, with keyhole arches, a well-proportioned dome on a crenulated base, and interlaced carved arabesques.

## MUSÉE DE MARRAKESH

**☎ 024 390911; www.museedemarrakech .ma; admission Dh40, with Medersa & Koubba Dh60; 9am-7pm;**

Once you've settled into a sofa in its *zellij*-bedecked *bhous* (seating nooks), mesmerised by the golden light of the courtyard and its burbling fountains, you might want to stay awhile – or forever. But it wasn't always so peaceful at this palace. Original owner Mehdi Mnebhi had a spectacular rise and fall as the minister of defence under Sultan Moulay Abdelaziz, who was first decorated by Queen Victoria then betrayed by England and forced to flee to Tangiers. Like most other nice digs in Marrakesh at the time, the palace was snatched up by colonial conspirator Pasha Glaoui. After independence it briefly became a girls' school, but

## ESSENTIAL BARGAINING BANTER

A little friendly banter brings better prices and good feelings all around. Here's what you need to know to bargain like a local:

| | |
|---|---|
| *asmeetek?* | What's your name? |
| *metsherrfin* | Honoured to meet you. |
| *kulshi bikher?* | Everything's good? |
| *labes, barakallahuafik/i* | Fine, bless you. |
| *saha labes?* | Your health is good? |
| *laliha labes?* | Your family's good? |
| *allah yrhem waldik/i . . .* | If it's no trouble . . . (when asking or receiving help; lit. 'May god protect your parents') |
| *wakha nshufha?* | May I look at it? |
| *makein mushkil* | No problem. |
| *bshhal?* | How much is it? |
| *akhir taman shhal?* | What's the last price? |
| *zhmaha li afak* | Please wrap it. |
| *allahyakhlef* | May it be returned to you. (when receiving money or hospitality) |
| *ma'asalama, sahbee* | With peace, my friend. |

it has since been restored by the Omar Benjelloun Foundation as a showplace for Moroccan traditional arts and travelling art shows. It usually displays European modern art at its kitschiest – which, given the palace's history, seems like fair play. See p22 for more.

### RAHBA QEDIMA
**off Souq Nejarine;** ⏲ 9am-8pm
Harry and the Hogwarts crowd probably shop here for school supplies. The Rahba Qedima is ringed with apothecaries who sell exotic and mysterious spell supplies to locals and traditional cosmetics to tourists, who eagerly dip a wet finger into clay pots of *aker* and smear it on their lips as rouge – apparently unaware that this stuff is made of ground-up insects.

# SHOP
### ABDELATIF INSTRUMENTS
*Musical Instruments*
**86 Souq Kchachbia, near Souq Haddadine;** ⏲ 9.30am-6pm
Musicians make pilgrimages to the lute-maker's souq to watch beautiful music in the making, and here you can glimpse *maâlem* (master craftsman) Sidi Abdelatif carving lutes, tambourines, *ginbris* (two-stringed banjos) and *ribabs* (single-stringed fiddles). Since you're buying straight from the artisan himself, you can customise

yours and get a better deal, too – music to every starving musician's ears.

### AIMAD ROI DES BABOUCHES *Fashion*
☎ 060 97471; Rue Biyyadine, 4th store on the right; ⏲ 9am-7pm
Quicker to catch on to new fashion trends than many other clothing shops in the souqs, Aimad also has a much more easygoing sales pitch. Recent styles include linen tunics edged with a crenulation motif you'll recognise from Koutoubia Minaret and well-lined *sabra* (cactus silk) slippers without the recently tanned scent you'll find in shops closer to the tanneries.

### BAB EL-KHEMIS MARKET *Market*
**Bab el-Khemis, Medina ramparts;** ⏲ 8am-noon Thu
Wonder where riads get all those old wooden doors, funky 1960s lawn chairs and Art Deco stained-glass windows? Follow the stampede of riad owners early Thursday morning to outside Bab el-Khemis (Thursday Gate), where a weekly market surfaces architectural salvage and other finds.

### BOB MUSIC *Musical Instruments*
☎ 066 745200; Rue Dabachi
In case you hadn't noticed the Bob Marley posters and music in shops

throughout the souqs, this store makes the Marrakesh-Jamaica connection even more obvious. Gnaoua musicians are quick to point out the similarity in some rhythmic patterns and tunes, but you can put this ethonomusicology theory to the test yourself: pick up some Gnaoua castanets or a drum in this shop, and try your own Gnaoua rendition of 'Redemption Song'. No matter how badly you play it, you're bound to make their day at Bob Music.

### ☐ CHAY ABDELHADI
*Homewares*
☎ 024 444412; 18 Kissariat della la Rue Nejjarine; ⏱ 10am-7pm
If you wish a genie would add some magic to your home décor – poof! – here's your dream pouf, in a range of shapes, colours and prices. The traditional round ones come embroidered, embossed and gilded, and the funky square ones are available outstitched, high-gloss and in rich natural shades. Prices vary by leather quality; the best is thick, durable and carefully tanned so the dye won't fade or rub off.

### ☐ CHEZ AZZEDINE
*Passimenterie*
☎ 065 241860; 13 Souq Stailia, near Souq Semmarine; ⏱ 9am-7pm
For small gifts, this place has all the trimmings. *Passimenterie* is

the art of trim, including tassels, braiding and ingenious knotting, and here the Moroccan tradition is turned into snazzy silk necklaces, knotted key rings, and grand curtain ties finished with two-foot-long tassels.

### ☐ COOPERATIVE ARTISANALE FEMMES DE MARRAKECH
*Moroccan Crafts*
☎ 024 378308; 67 Souq Kchachbia
Fair trade never looked so stylish. When Souad (opposite) and nine Marrakshi women artisans wound up with overstock and design ideas from a big American order for snappy, linen-cotton blend tunics, they realised they could skip the middleman and sell their own modern designs right in Marrakesh. With a small grant, they've set up this boutique and made connections with other cooperatives whose work they sell at low, fixed prices in a small annex. Products include sustainably harvested thuya wood bowls from Essaouira, Safi tea sets and small Middle Atlas rugs.

### ☐ ENFIN *Fashion*
☎ 024 356467; Souq Chkaira, near Souq Cherratine; ⏱ 10am-6.30pm Mon-Sat
Trim, modern, hottie tunics for men in sumptuous materials and colours: deep red linen, ivory with black trim around the neck, black

### Souad Boudeiry
*Medina fashionista and fair trade trendsetter for Cooperative Artisanale Femmes de Marrakech (opposite)*

**Favourite places in the Medina** Besides my neighbourhood? The Djemaa el-Fna is its own city, and you can take it all in from Café Argana (p75) and Café du Grand Balcon (p76) – it's always fascinating, no matter how many times you see it. The souqs are a theatre, and every day is a new act. From one word, these guys can make a joke! **Marrakshiyya fashion statements** The modern kaftan has smart details: colour contrasts, or no sleeves, or a distinctive neckline. I don't wear *djellabas* [robes] often, but a well-tailored one makes great evening wear. **The look for men** Traditionally, it's an embroidered *tráa* [large, square tunic with slit arm-holes] and bright yellow *smata* [slippers] – but now maybe with jeans. **Marrakshiyyas on the move** The women's revolution is already here: we're in every profession, we're in Parliament, we're not hiding. We have the same problems as any other working women, but we know our rights and we're claiming them.

raw silk with a single off-centre grey stripe. Prices aren't cheap, but with the right bargaining banter you can get better deals here than in Enfin's factory outlet in Sidi Ghanem (p46). The pink-and-black boutique and sharply dressed staff are incongruously glitzy for the raw, hardworking northern section of the souqs – but that's what makes Enfin so quintessentially Marrakesh.

### 🏠 MICHI *Fashion & Homewares*
☎ 061 864407; http://michimaroc.ex blog.jp (in Japanese); 19/21 Souq Lakhachbia

Berber wabisabi is the design ethic at Michi, a creative partnership of Japanese Marrakesh resident Masayoshi Ishida and Marrakshi master craftsmen. Together they've created a look that combines natural materials, spare forms and a whimsical sense of humour: woven raffia wing-tip shoes, a long-handled mug with a tiny orange-wood spoon, flour-sack tote bags lined with basketry. Even with your most winsome bargaining behaviour, Michi is more expensive than most souq shops: staff know you won't find this stuff elsewhere.

### 🏠 MOHAMMED BEN EL-HAIR *Carpets*
284 Draze Souq el-Kebir, near Musée de Marrakesh; ⏰ 9am-7pm

Mt Everest is overrated; the most thrilling mountain to scale is the one of colourful Berber carpets in this tiny shop. Charming elderly proprietor Abu Mohammed ushers you in with a smile and mint tea, then waves towards the mountain with a single word: 'Democracy!' This is your invitation to clamber up, and pull down whatever carpets appeal to you. The prices are more than democratic; they're downright proletarian.

### 🏠 SIDI AHMAD GABAZ STUCCO *Moroccan Crafts*
2 Souq Shaaria; ⏰ 9.30am-6pm Sat-Thu, 9am-noon Fri

Like any visitor with 20/20 vision, you may already be awestruck by the stucco detail up the street at the Ali ben Youssef Medersa – and this is your chance to take home a piece of the stucco action. Sidi Ahmad carves traditional geometric and floral designs right in his shop as well as sweet nothings in French, but with a day's turnaround he will very graciously carve your house number or whatever you like in English…just don't get any four-letter ideas, you naughty people.

## 🍴 EAT

### 🍴 BEN YOUSSEF FOOD STALL QISSARIA
*Marrakesh Specialities*                                          $
off Souq Shaaria, near Koubba Ba'adiyn; ⏰ 11.30am-3.30pm

Just around the corner from the Koubba Ba'adiyn is a labyrinth of *qissarias* lined with stalls serving tagines, steaming snails, and the occasional stewed sheep's head hot off the Buddha gas burner. Tourists at food stalls in the Djemaa el-Fna may think they're being adventurous, but the *qissarias* are where the real action is. Eat whatever looks fresh and tasty, even if you have to wait for a free stool.

### CAFÉ DE MUSÉE DE MAR-RAKESH *Café & Sandwiches* $
☎ 024 390911; Musée de Marrakesh; 9am-7pm;

Rest those museum legs at the Musée's artistically inclined courtyard café, where you can refuel for the return trip through the souqs with a soft drink or strong coffee, respectable tuna sandwiches on fresh bread with olives, and a generous serving of art by local emerging artists. The ideal vantage point to watch the faithful heading to their mosque, nearby shopkeepers trying tactics on prospective buyers, and dazed shoppers emerging from the souqs.

### DAR TIMTAM *Moroccan Á La Carte* $
☎ 024 391446; Zinkat Rahba, near Rahba Qedima; 11.30am-4pm;
V

Don't feel daunted by the dimly lit restaurant through the front door – take a right out the back and into the stately sanctuary of this 18th-century riad's innermost courtyard, where rejuvenating mint tea and tasty lunches are served by chatty staff. The generous assortment of salads are a feast for Dh65, and you'll feel miles away from the souqs here among the songbirds.

### LE FOUNDOUK *Moroccan Fusion* $$
☎ 024 378190; www.foundouk.com; 55 Souq el-Fez, near Ali ben Youssef Medersa; noon-1am

Push past the studded doors and you've entered a movie where the lighting is perfect, the sets

Setting the mood at Le Foundouk

NEIGHBOURHOODS

CENTRAL SOUQS & DERB DEBACHI

are breathtaking and everyone is good-looking. This 18th-century riad sets the scene in shades of ivory, black and deep purple, crowned with a spidery iron chandelier straight out of a Tim Burton movie. Silk-costumed waiters glide from one private seating nook to the next like butterflies, bearing fresh strawberry juice, Casa beer and champagne Bellinis with fresh peach juice. Square henna lamps with fringes made from cloves set the mood for a savoury *bastilla* (pigeon pie), which is so much easier to appreciate when it's not the third of five courses. Don't miss a trip to the terrace for your establishing shot of Marrakesh.

# DRINK
## CAFÉ DES ÉPICES *Café*
☎ 024 391770; Rahba Qedima; ☾ 8am-9pm

Grab a prime spot above the healers and potion-dealers of the Rahba Qedima and watch the magic happen as you sip a reviving caffeinated beverage. The young Marrakshi staff are hip and easygoing, there's free wi-fi, and if you linger over mint tea long enough, the rooftop terrace offers a sunset view of the souqs. Salads and sandwiches are fresh but bland – all the more reason to skip to the sweets.

One fresh OJ coming up, at Café des Épices

# PLAY

## BAIN D'OR *Hammam*

Derb Zaouiat Lakhdar, near Ali ben Youssef Medersa; men Dh7, women Dh7.5, gommage extra; ⏱ men 6-11am & 8.30pm-midnight, women 11am-8.30pm

This is your friendly neighbourhood public hammam, small and lovely with stuccoed detail and sunlight filtering through the dome. As at all public hammams, bring your own plastic mat, flip-flops, towel and a change of undies – you'll be expected to wear yours.

# > BAB DOUKKALA & DAR EL-BACHA

Just out of earshot of Djemaa el-Fna crowds and the hustle of the souqs, this neighbourhood is a prime place to see what the Medina is like in its downtime. Women linger to chat outside community hammams, kids pull on parents' hands as they pass carts loaded with sesame sweets, and students throng cybercafés to make kissy faces at their latest love interests via webcam. Take a cue from the locals and relax, already: right behind the major routes and food souqs you'll find tranquil riads and fabulous restaurants, and a short walk away are the clubs and restaurants of Nouvelle Ville. Through Bab Doukkala (Doukkala Gate) is the busy CTM bus station, and coming back from clubs late at night you'll want to know where you're going to avoid minor hassle. But generally the neighbourhood looks after its own, and within a day or two of staying here and saying hello to the lady who feeds local cats on her front stoop, that includes you.

## BAB DOUKKALA & DAR EL-BACHA

### 🏠 SHOP
Association
  al Kawtar ..................... 1  D5
Bab Doukkala
  food souq ..................... 2  B2
Boutique Noir
  d'Ivoire ........................ 3  C1
Mohammed Rida
  ben Zouine .................. 4  D3

Mustapha Blaoui ............ 5  D3
Pharmacie Koutoubia .... 6  D5

### 🍽 EAT
Dar Moha ........................ 7  D3
La Maison Arabe
  Restaurant ................. 8  C3
Le Pavillon ..................... 9  B3
Riad 72 ......................... 10  C3

### 🍸 DRINK
La Maison Arabe Bar ....(see 8)

### ⭐ PLAY
Hammam Bab
  Doukkala ................... 11  C3
Hammam
  Dar el-Bacha ............. 12  D5
Maison Arabe .............. (see 8)

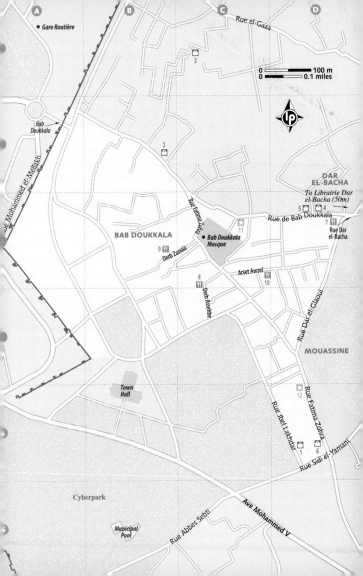

**Gare Routière**

A

B

C Rue el-Gaza

D

Bab Doukkala

Rue Mohammed et-Zheltakh

3

2

DAR EL-BACHA

To Librairie Dar el-Bacha (50m)

5 4

Rue de Bab Doukkala

7

Rue Dar el-Bacha

Rue Fatima Zohra

BAB DOUKKALA

Bab Doukkala Mosque

11

9 Derb Zaouia

8 Derb Assehbe

Arset Awzel

10

Rue Dar el-Chaoui

MOUASSINE

Town Hall

Rue Jbel Lakhdar

Rue Fatima Zohra

12

1 6

Rue Sidi el-Yamani

Cyberpark

Ave Mohammed V

Rue Abbes Sebti

Municipal Pool

0 —————— 100 m
0 —————— 0.1 miles

#  SHOP

## ASSOCIATION AL KAWTAR
*Homewares*

☎ 024 385695; 35 Rue Jbel Lakhdar;
🕐 10am-7pm

Bring some *baraka* (good vibes) to your table with hand-embroidered table linens in spare, striking designs, all made at a nonprofit vocational training and daycare centre for disabled women and their children. Exquisitely edged pillow cases, hand towels and napkins make lovely feel-good gifts at perfectly reasonable fixed prices.

## BAB DOUKKALA FOOD SOUQ *Food*

Rue Fatima Zohra, btwn Bab Doukkala Mosque & Bab Doukkala bus station;
🕐 9am-8pm

Less touristy than the central souqs and easier to navigate, this neighbourhood market is a prime spot to pick up spices, preserved lemons, earthenware tagines and other gourmet goodies, plus fresh fruit and baked goods.

## BOUTIQUE NOIR D'IVOIRE
*Fashion & Beauty Products*

☎ 024 380975; www.noir-d-ivoire.com; Riad Noir d'Ivoire, 31 Derb Jedid Bab Doukkala; 🕐 usually noon-6pm & by appointment

Sure, you could spend days digging in the souqs for elusive treasures, wired on mint tea – or you could just head directly to this boutique, where style trendsetter Jill Fechtman has thoughtfully done all the footwork for you. Find sought-after botanical Sens de Marrakesh products, as well as custom cloaks and eveningwear by Mohammed Rida ben Zouine in the riad's trademark black and ivory. You can even enjoy a cocktail in the courtyard afterward.

## LIBRAIRIE DAR EL-BACHA
*Bookshop*

☎ 024 391973; 14 Rue Dar el-Bacha;
🕐 9am-1pm & 3-7.30pm

A fine selection of cookbooks, art books, and postcards, plus stamps to send them and some wonderful antique Moroccan stamps to take to all your philatelist friends back home. Bookshop owner Noureddine Tilsaghani is also a photographer, and you can pick up some of his atmospheric shots of Marrakesh here. There's a fantastic selection of Moroccan literature and poetry in (mostly French) translation.

## MOHAMMED RIDA BEN ZOUINE *Fashion*

☎ 024 385056; 142 Rte Arset Aouzal;
🕐 9am-7.30pm

Saville Row tailors would bite their thimbled thumbs with envy at Ben Zouine's custom hand-finished men's shirts, curve-skimming linen dresses with handmade silk closures and snappy hooded jackets in 'Moroccan cashmere' (thick combed-cotton flannel). Sidi Mohammed keeps tabs on the latest men's suit styles from Belgium, and can make you a slimming, bitter chocolate brown suit with a sneaky orange lining that Dries van Noten might admire.

###  MUSTAPHA BLAOUI
*Homewares*

☎ 024 385240; 142-4 Rue de Bab Doukkala; ⏰ 9am-8pm

The next best thing to taking your riad home would be to take home all those fabulous furnishings – and with Mustapha Blaoui's generous shipping policy and stock of everything from hand-embroidered coverlets to inlaid rolltop desks, that's actually possible. Some items are imported from India, so if you want to bring home a Marrakshi speciality, just ask the easygoing staff to point you toward the locally produced goods.

### PHARMACIE KOUTOUBIA
*Pharmacy & Beauty Products*

☎ 024 381072; Ave Fatima Zohra, cnr Rue Sidi el-Yamani

All the essentials you forgot to bring are here, plus fragrant

In stitches: Mohammed Rida Ben Zouine

Nectarôme skin- and hair-care products from the organic gardens in nearby Ourika Valley. If you're not feeling your best, just tell the sharp young pharmacist what's wrong – she'll point out the best pharmaceutical or homeopathic cures for what ails you.

## 🍴 EAT

### 🍴 DAR MOHA
*Moroccan Fusion*                    $$$

☎ 024 386400; www.darmoha.ma; 81 Rue Dar el-Bacha; ⏰ 12-3pm & 7.30pm-midnight Tue-Sun; Ⓥ

Thrones are overrated; the most coveted spot in Marrakesh is at chef Mohammed Fedal's table. This Marrakshi maverick gives tastebuds a fresh outlook with clever variations on Moroccan ingredients: duck breast infused with argan oil, a *'zellij'* (mosaic) of grilled seasonal vegetables with Berber herbs, a pear topped with saffron sorbet and toasted almonds. The set Dh220 lunch menu is a more traditional feast, with dish after irresistible dish of orange flower–scented cucumbers and spice-rubbed grilled lamb chops. Alcohol served.

### LA MAISON ARABE RESTAURANT *Moroccan* $$$

☎ 024 387010; www.lamaisonarabe .com; 1 Derb Assehbe; ⏱ 7.30pm-midnight; ✷ V

La Maison Arabe was serving Moroccan fine dining decades before other riads, and viva la *diffa* (feast) difference: here the focus is on the food and company, get-cozy booth seating, excellent classical Andalusian musicians instead of cheesy belly dancers, and the humble Marrakshi *tangia* elevated to a main attraction. Even the scaled-down Dh330 menu qualifies as a feast, so make an evening of it – and tomorrow you can take classes here to learn how it's done. Alcohol served.

### LE PAVILLON *French* $$$

☎ 024 387040; www.restaurantle pavillon.com; 47 Derb Zaouia, near Bab Doukkala Mosque; ⏱ 8pm-midnight Wed-Mon

Just when you think you've taken a wrong turn, a lantern-bearer appears to guide you down the long alley to this lovely riad and its fig tree–filled garden of Gallic delights with Moroccan touches. The duck breast with peaches is especially tender and juicy with the peach flavour adding a zing; the fish is flaky and delicately scented with local herbs. The downside is the wine selection: the house wine by the glass we tried was tannic with a vague aftertaste of tyres, so you'll have to spring for the overpriced wines by the bottle. Could be worse, couldn't it.

### RIAD 72 *Moroccan* $$

☎ 024 387629; www.riad72.com; Riad 72, 72 Arest Awzel; ⏱ lunch, dinner by reservation; V

Like a model with insane metabolism, this slinky Italian-run guesthouse has a passion for refined homestyle Moroccan dishes. The eggplant caviar makes Beluga seem unoriginal, and potatoes are transformed by a tangy herbal treatment that might make a great facial, too. Go for lunch around the incense-wafting courtyard fountain – the incense can be put out if it's cramping your culinary style – or book ahead for dinner atop the highest terrace around. Alcohol served.

# DRINK

## LA MAISON ARABE BAR *Bar*

☎ 024 387010; www.lamaisonarabe
.com; 1 Derb Assehbe; ☒ 8pm-1am; ☒
It could be the 20-year single malt
scotch talking, but fellow drinkers
tend to look dashing reclining on
leather club chairs by the fireplace
within these hand-carved wood
walls. The fusion tapas vacillate
between bland and deep-fried
beyond all recognition; stick to
drinks and save your appetite
for La Maison Arabe Restaurant
(opposite).

 # PLAY

## HAMMAM BAB DOUKKALA
*Hammam*

**Rue de Bab Doukkala, northeast cnr Bab
Doukkala Mosque; admission Dh7.50;
☒ women noon-7pm, men from 8pm**
A simple, lovely community hammam that dates from the 17th century. Pass through the cedar-wood
changing room and you'll reach
the inner sanctum; here light filters
through star-shaped holes in the
dome, steam rises from the floor,
and the mostly local patrons rest
against stately columns while waiting for a *gommage* (body scrub)
exfoliating treatment.

## HAMMAM DAR EL-BACHA
*Hammam*

**20 Rue Fatima Zohra; admission men
Dh7, women Dh7.50; ☒ men 7am-1pm,
women 1-9pm**
The city's most historic public
hammam has domed ceilings
so high you'll wonder how the
place ever steams up – and yet it
has for over a century. A massage
costs from Dh50 to Dh100, and
*gommage* just Dh15. If the skin-
sloughing ever approaches the
blood-vessel-breaking point, just
say, *'Shwiyya shwiyya'* ('Easy does
it'). Bring your public hammam kit
(see p143) including dry undies.

## MAISON ARABE *Hammam*

☎ 024 387010; www.lamaisonarabe
.com; La Maison Arabe Riad, 1 Derb
Assehbe; Ⓟ
Slip into something more comfortable, like this snug *tadelakt*
(polished plaster) hammam with
vaulted ceilings and baths deli-
ciously scented with local herbs
and minerals instead of cloying
floral scents. The hammam comes
with *gommage* and *rhassoul* (mud
scalp rub; Dh350) and hair removal
is done here the time-honoured
way, with thread and some very
fast hands.

# > MOUASSINE

At least 500 years old, and yet it hasn't aged a day. The Mouassine reveals traces of ancient Marrakesh in its stately riads, mosques and neighbourhood fountain, yet it stays current with cutting-edge design and cosmopolitan cuisine. This is an ideal place to stay in a riad given the large number of historic homes in the neighbourhood and its location near the Djemaa el-Fna, souqs, and taxis to Nouvelle Ville. Because it's so central and busy, it's safe and easy to navigate for women and solo travellers – yet there's still plenty to discover. Spend a morning exploring Mouassine souqs and *fondouqs* (ancient artisans' studio complexes), where you might glimpse innovative designs destined for the Mouassine's stylish boutiques. The Mouassine offers prices that beat Nouvelle Ville for well-crafted, original lamps, handbags, jewellery and carpets. Chill out between shops in courtyard cafés, and dine in style at your riad or some of the city's best Moroccan restaurants.

# MOUASSINE

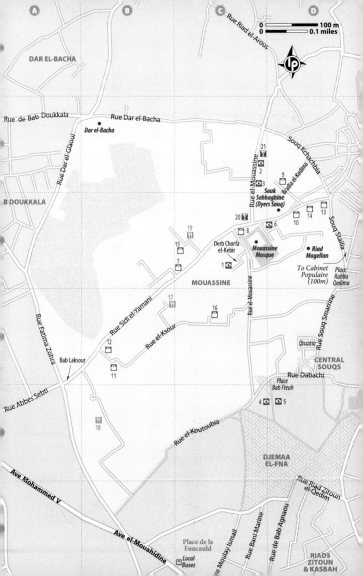

# SEE

## DAR CHÉRIFA

☎ 024 426463; www.marrakech-riads
.net; 8 Derb Chorfa el-Kebir, near Rue el-
Mouassine; admission free, tea Dh15-25;
⏰ noon-7pm

Revive souq-sore eyes with a
visit to this serene, impeccably
restored late-15th-century Saadian riad, where tea and coffee
is served with contemporary art
and literature. Stop by for shows
by local artists, lovely illustrated
editions of Arabic poetry in French
translation, and saffron tea on
the rooftop terrace. Don't miss
concerts and art openings at this
cultural centre, or you'll be left
wandering the streets wondering
where everyone else went.

## FONDOUQS

off Djemaa el-Fna, near Place Bab Fteuh
& 196 Rue el-Mouassine, near Café Arabe;
⏰ usually 9am-7pm, individual artisan's
studios vary

Since medieval times, these creative courtyard complexes featured
ground-floor artisans' workshops

The art of teatime at Dar Chérifa

and rented rooms upstairs – and from their flux of artisans and adventurers emerged the inventive culture of modern-day Marrakesh. Only 140 *fondouqs* remain in the Medina, including notable ones near Place Bab Ftueh and one on Rue el-Mouassine featured in the film *Hideous Kinky*. The king recently announced a Dh40 million plan to spruce up 98 *fondouqs,* so now's the time to see them in all their shop-worn glory.

### MOUASSINE FOUNTAIN

**Rue Sidi el-Yamani, near Rue el-Mouassine**
The Medina had 40 fountains at the start of the 20th century, and each neighbourhood relied on its own for water for cooking, public baths, orchards and gardens. The Mouassine Fountain is a classic example, with carved wood details and continued use as a neighbourhood wool-drying area and gossip source.

# SHOP

### ARTISANT EL KOUTOUBIA
*Lighting*
☎ 024 427106; 55 Rue Sidi el-Yamani; ⏱ 9am-7pm
Mood lighting is a Moroccan speciality, and here you have it: turquoise *tadelakt* (polished plaster) table lamps to brighten end tables, wall sconces for dramatic entrances, and grand pierced-

metal chandeliers to add dazzle to dining. Shipping is tricky, but Aziza will pack purchases for your flight home.

### ASSOUSS COOPERATIVE D'ARGANE *Gourmet & Beauty Products*
**cnr Rue el-Mouassine & Rue Sidi el-Yamani;** ⏱ **9am-1pm & 3-7pm Sat-Thu, 9am-noon Fri**
Argan oil is the most effective cosmetic and tasty gourmet treat ever to pass through the business end of a goat, and it's the speciality of this women's cooperative. Get yours pure and straight from the source at this women-run shop, and reward artisanal producers for tough work sorting argan pits from goat dung, cracking the rock-hard pits open, and pressing oil from the nut. The richly emollient end product has long protected Sahara-exposed skin, and now European cosmetics companies use it as the secret botanical ingredient in high-end creams.

### CABINET POPULAIRE
*Beauty Products*
☎ 024 426298; 99 Souq Nejarine; ⏱ 10am-7pm
Stop and taste the rosewater, anoint yourself with healing essential oils and, on hot days, kindly Sidi Aboubida will pour a little cooling orange-flower water

on your head. This is a full-service Berber pharmacy and cosmetics counter, with roots, powders and lotions in folk-art packaging for any conceivable complaint, from spots to shyness. Prices are set, and very popular indeed.

### CHEZ LES NOMADES
*Carpets*
☎ 024 442259; www.chezlesnomades .com; 32-34 Bradia El Kedima, near Souq Sebbaghine (Dyers' Souq); 🕙 8.30am-7.30pm

A wide selection of antique and modern Berber carpets, reasonable prices, and a pleasant all-round carpet-shopping experience. Salah will explain (in perfect English) key differences in motifs, regions and quality with a variety of carpet types, then pull out carpets in whatever style and size appeals to you. Enjoy the tea and the education, without the usual hustle; here the selection speaks for itself.

### CREATION CHEZ LAMINE
*Homewares*
☎ 024 427517; 17 Souq des Teinturiers; 🕙 10am-7pm

You can't take a hammam home with you, but you can give your bath a Marrakshi makeover with Chez Lamine's tasselled *tadelakt* toothbrush holders and hammered tin mirrors. Most tinware and *tadelakt* items are for decorative use; for kitchenware, ask which pieces are safe for food.

### KIFKIF
*Accessories & Homewares*
☎ 061 082041; www.kifkifbystef .com; 8 Rue el-Ksour, near Bab Laksour; 🕙 10am-8pm

Mirrors made of Moroccan sardine cans, silver rings with interchangeable felt baubles and satchels made of striped awning vinyl: Kifkif employs Marrakesh's hippest artisans to create original designs that are often copied but never quite equalled elsewhere in the

Salah explains Berber symbols at Chez les Nomades

### Said Ben Azzouz

*Former London commodities trader returned to run the family antiques business, Tresors de Mille et Une Nuit (p103)*

**Why antiques?** I have a passion for arts and antiques. When I get home, I take out my canvas, or get out an enamelled egg I'm working on. The income's definitely not the same as in commodities, but there's also beauty to consider. **Antiques savvy** Study an antique before you buy it – its region and style – because some very good replicas were made 50 to 60 years ago. You can make sales contingent on an expert pinning down a specific date in a certificate of authenticity. **Best bargaining tip** What, and give it away? [laughs] Just look the person you're dealing with in the eye, and be sincere. If they don't respond in kind, walk away. **Not at any price** One item I regret selling to this day is a very old Torah. Jewish artefacts are part of our heritage as Moroccans, and to me it's a symbolic part of our history that should stay with us here in Marrakesh.

souqs. Great stuff for kids too, especially soft, striped baby *djellabas* (robes).

## KULCHI *Fashion*

☎ 062 649783; 1bis Rue el-Ksour; ⏰ 9.30am-1pm & 3-7.30pm Mon-Sat
Now you know where Marrakesh clubbers get their chic looks. This local designer mixes trade-route African influences with a Marrakshi sense of humour: mod cocktail dresses in Senegalese Pop Art prints, sleek handbags made from recycled signage and come-hither kaftans in diaphanous fabrics. Prices aren't cheap, but less than you'd pay for original designs back home. Check out the sister boutique inside Le Comptoir (p55).

## L'ART DU BAIN SAVONNERIE ARTISANALE *Beauty Products*

☎ 068 445942; www.lartdubain.com; Souq Lebbading, near Souq Sebbaghine; ⏰ 9.30am-7.30pm
An abundance of fragrant, artisanal bath products delight the senses: pyramids of handmade palm oil soaps with organic bergamot and vetiver; towers of shaving soap with soothing Moroccan mint; and shelves of argan oil from an Essaouira cooperative, in tassel-topped bottles. Organic, artisanal soaps cost just Dh30 to

Dh50 (fixed price), and gifts come sprinkled with rosebuds and star anise and tied with raffia.

## MASROURE ABDILLAH *Accessories & Moroccan Crafts*

☎ 064 817254; 53 Souq Lebbadine, near Souq Sebbaghine; ⏰ 9am-7.30pm
It usually takes decades to earn the title *maâlem* (master craftsperson), but young Masroure earns the title the hard way, pounding wool with *savon noir* (black soap) into felt. He then moulds it into seamless slippers, baubles for necklaces, and sturdy tote bags. Masroure's felt flowers come in snappy shades of natural brown, bright orange and splashy hot pink, and make groovy brooches, hatpins and everlasting bouquets.

## MINISTERO DEL GUSTO *Art, Homewares & Fashion*

☎ 024 426455; www.ministerodelgusto .com; 22 Derb El Azouz, off Rue Sidi el-Yamani, near Rue el-Mouassine; ⏰ 10am-1pm Mon-Sat, afternoons by appointment
You may have to elbow David Bowie and Iman out of the way to snap up that Moroccan Pop Art painting. Stop by to ogle the Gaudí-gone-Berber décor, and score custom-designed accessories such as hand-carved lemonwood cutlery plus vintage finds – includ-

ing some killer vintage party dresses on the mezzanine. Call ahead, or you might find the place closed for a fashion mag photo shoot.

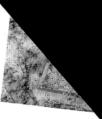

### TRESORS DE MILLE ET UNE NUIT *Antiques*

☎ 024 440931; 8 Derb Sania, off Rue el-Ksour; ⏰ 9am-9pm

An antique-hunting couple from Philadelphia wander through the unmarked door of this family riad for a quick snoop, and within minutes they're earnestly discussing shipping containers. Happens all the time to Said, whose family has been in the décor and antiques business for generations and has the stockpiled treasures to prove it: sand-worn Berber doors, rare Tuareg amulets, Art Deco lithographs and a striking armoire inlaid with camel bone.

# EAT
### KSAR ESSAOUSSAN
*Moroccan Fixed-price Feast* $$$

☎ 024 440632; 3 Derb El Messaoudy-enne, off Rue el-Ksour; ⏰ 7.30-11pm Mon-Sat

For seasonal fixed-price feasts and good value in an 18th-century riad, follow the lantern-carrier here from Rue el-Ksour. Meals start at Dh350, including an aperitif, wine and mint tea. Enjoy your aperitif by the rooftop fountain, almost

lah ben Hessaien, near Bab...
⏰ 7.30-11pm Wed-Mon, reservations required

Dar Moha and Al Fassia have the edge for á la carte menus, but Tobsil is still top-notch for prix-fixe feasts in an intimate riad. As Gnaoua musicians play in the courtyard, up to 50 guests (no tour groups here) indulge in button-popping five-course menus with aperitifs and wine pairings for Dh550. No excess glitz and belly dancers distract from upstanding *meze* (starters), *bastilla* (pigeon pie), tagines (yes, that's plural) and couscous, capped off with mint tea, fresh fruit and Moroccan pastries.

### VILLA FLORE
*Moroccan Fusion* $$

☎ 024 391700; www.villa-flore.com; 4 Derb Azzouz; ⏰ 12.30-3pm & 7.30-11pm

Some come for meltingly tender lamb and duck; some for the relaxed black-and-white riad setting that's snazzy as a tuxedo and

Relax with a coffee in a riad garden: Bougainvillea

comfy as a *djellaba*; and others, it must be admitted, for that blindingly handsome maitre d'. But the best draw is the Dh50 Moroccan salad, three perfect circles of Moroccan *meze* that elevate lowly aubergines and peppers to major sensations with aromatic ras al-hanout spice.

## ☕ DRINK

### ▼ BOUGAINVILLEA *Café*
☎ 024 441111; 33 Rue el-Mouassine;
⏰ 11am-10pm;

No matter how your souq bargaining sessions went today, good cheer is at hand in this upbeat purple riad practically wallpapered with whimsical abstract paintings of the Medina. Unwind with tea, coffee or soft drinks in the garden near the wall-o-water fountain, or in cosy *bhous* (seating nooks). The sandwiches are serviceable and the service is friendly, if not fast.

### ▼ CAFÉ ARABE *Café-Bar*
☎ 024 429728; www.cafearabe.com;
184 Rue el-Mouassine; ⏰ 9am-midnight;
♿ Ⅴ ♿

Gloat over souq purchases with cocktails on the roof or alongside the Zen-*zellij* (mosaic) courtyard fountain. Wine prices here are down to earth for such a stylish place, and you can order half-bottles of better Moroccan wines such as the peppery red Siroua S. The food is bland but the company isn't – artists and designers flock here – so grab a bite and join the conversation.

# > RIADS ZITOUN & KASBAH

Ultramodern and ancient are never far apart in Marrakesh, as you'll discover when you bunk in among the monuments at a trendy local riad, get the latest spa treatments at a Kasbah hammam or troll boutiques for original designs along Rue Riad Zitoun el-Kedim. Visitors emerge dazed from neighbourhood derbs, gobsmacked by riads and palaces that are floor-to-ceiling showplaces of Marrakshi creativity. To the east of Riad Zitoun el-Jedid are three marvellous Marrakesh mansions: the elegantly refined Dar Si Said, now a museum that shows how Moroccans make an art of everyday life, from doorknobs to daggers; Maison Tiskiwin, home and living history museum of anthropologist Bert Flint; and Bahia Palace, where harems once held court and Mohammed VI still holds royal parties for rappers. Near the Bahia Palace is the Mellah, once the largest Jewish quarter in North Africa. With 20th-century emigration to Europe, the neighbourhood became mostly Muslim, and it's now called Hay-Es-Salam – but the neighbourhood's ancient character remains, as do its myriad contributions to Marrakshi society, craft and commerce.

## RIADS ZITOUN & KASBAH

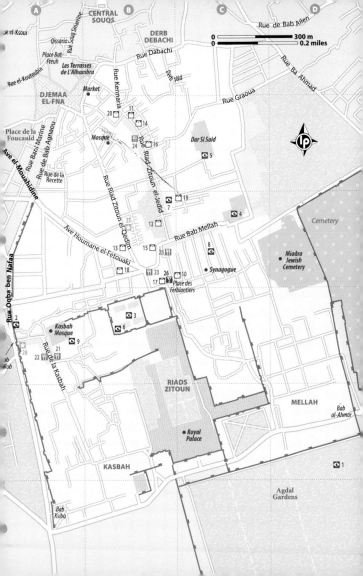

#  SEE

## 🔘 AGDAL GARDENS

**south of the Royal Palace, Kasbah; 🕑 3-6.30pm Fri, noon-6pm Sun**
Moroccan sultans have greeted dignitaries here for eight centuries, among fragrant fruit and olive orchards and reflecting pools stocked with psychic carp that sense you and your bread crusts coming. The gardens still serve ceremonial purposes, so they're only open weekends and when the king isn't in residence.

## 🔘 BAB AGNAOU

**exterior of Medina ramparts, 20m north of Bab er-Rob**
One of the 20 gates in the Marrakesh city walls, this 12th-century 'gate of the Gnaoua' (named for the sub-Saharan slaves who served the sultan) was one of the first stone monuments in Marrakesh and a triumph of Marrakshi artisanship. From afar the bas-relief appears much deeper than it actually is, due to a sophisticated trompe l'oeil effect. The bluish-gold-green colour of its Guéliz stone seems to change like a mood ring according to the time of the day, the heat and, perhaps, the city's disposition.

## 🔘 BADI PALACE

**near Place des Ferblantiers; admission Dh10, incl Koutobia Minbar Dh20; 🕑 8.30am-12pm & 2.30-6pm**

When 16th-century Sultan Ahmed el-Mansour was paving his palace with gold, turquoise and crystal, his jester wisecracked, 'It'll make a beautiful ruin'. That fool was a prophet: 75 years later the place was looted. Hard to picture the former glories of the now-barren courtyard, and the next-door garden is a royal mess with the king's security equipment – but the stork's-eye view atop the ramparts and periodic concerts here are musts.

## 🔘 BAHIA PALACE

**☎ 024 389564; Rue Riad Zitoun el-Jedid; admission Dh10; 🕑 8.30-11.45am & 2.30-5.45pm Mon-Thu, Sat & Sun, 8.30-11.30am & 3-5.45pm Fri; 👶 🚻**
Modern special-effects wizardry can't beat the optical effects of intricate stucco work and polychrome *zellij* (mosaic) topped by painted, inlaid woodwork ceilings. It took 14 years to achieve this effect in the late 19th century, and you can picture the intrigues that unfolded here back then: subjects pleading for clemency in the Court d'Honneur; courtesans courting royal attention in romantic gardens or hiding from them in private harem nooks; and enemies and wives of the Grand Vizier stripping the palace bare of its opulent furnishings before his body was cold. The entrance is near Place des Ferblantiers. See p17 for more.

Making a grand entrance: Bab Agnaou, one of the ancient gates into the city

### DAR SI SAID

☎ 024 389564; Rue Kennaria, near Rue Riad Zitoun el-Jedid; admission Dh30; ☺ 9am-noon & 3-6pm Wed-Mon; ♿

A monument to Moroccan *maâlems* (master craftsmen), the Dar Si Said highlights Marrakesh's graceful riad architecture and local craftsmanship – though artisans from Fez must be credited for the spectacular painted woodwork in the domed wedding chamber upstairs. Don't miss the door collection on the ground floor, painted musicians' balconies on the first, and the vaguely threatening kitchen implements on the second, plus views over the lovely *zellij* harem courtyard (currently undergoing restoration). See p20 for more.

### KOUTOUBIA MINBAR

Badi Palace; admission Dh20 incl Badi Palace; ☺ 8.30am-12pm & 2.30-6pm

Not to be confused with an ordinary staircase or a hotel beverage dispensary, this minbar (pulpit) is the Koutoubia's 12th-century prayer pulpit. With intricately

RIADS ZITOUN & KASBAH

carved cedar wood steps and minute gold, silver and ivory marquetry, this minbar is a credit to Cordoban craftsmanship under Moroccan rule and *maâlem* Aziz – the Metropolitan Museum of Art restoration uncovered his signature under the inlay.

**◉ MAISON TISKIWIN**
**☎ 024 389192; 8 Rue de la Bahia; admission Dh15; ⏰ 9am-12.30pm & 3-5.30pm**

Travel to Timbuktu and back again, via the private art collection of Dutch anthropologist Bert Flint. Each room represents a region of Morocco with indigenous crafts, from well-travelled Tuareg leather camel saddles to fine Middle Atlas carpets – the gold standard by which to judge the ones in the souqs. See if you can spot such recurring motifs as the *khamsa* (hand of Fatima) and the Southern

I'll tell you a bit of a story about that: guide at Saadian tombs

cross, the constellation that guided desert travellers.

## MELLAH

**east on Rue Riad Zitoun el-Jedid, south of the Bahia Palace**
In the narrow derbs of the city's historic Jewish quarter are the tallest mud-brick buildings in Marrakesh, with cross-alley chats in progress through wrought-iron Mellah balconies. Some doors are embellished with six-pointed stars and menorahs, and you may be guided towards the local synagogue and the Miaâra (Jewish cemetery), where guardians request donations from visitors for upkeep. But to see the living legacy of Mellah artisans and spice traders, check out the Place des Ferblantiers, Grand Bijouterie and Mellah Market.

## SAADIAN TOMBS

**Rue de la Kasbah, near Kasbah Mosque; admission Dh10; ⏰ 8.30-11.45am & 2.30-5.45pm; ♿**
Elvis Presley's tastes seem restrained compared with those of Sultan Ahmed al-Mansour, who spared no expense on his tomb, importing Italian Carrara marble and gilding honeycomb *muqarnas* (stalactite-type stone carving) archways with pure gold. The sultan played favourites even in death, keeping princes handy in the Chamber of the Three Niches, and relegating to garden plots

chancellors and wives – all of which are overshadowed by his mother's splendid mausoleum. See p15 for more.

 SHOP

### AYA'S *Fashion*
☎ 024 383428; www.ayasmarrakech.com; 11bis Derb Jedid Bab Mellah; ⏰ 9.30am-7pm Mon-Thu & Sat, 1-7pm Fri
Deluxe, hand-embroidered designer fashions worthy of a royal reception are offered here, from chocolate brown linen tunics with geometric, sky-blue embroidery to striped-silk kaftans in jewel tones with wide black silk borders straight out of a Matisse painting. They're not cheap, but not a king's ransom, either – and unlike the chunky jewellery and leather slippers, you won't find similar designs elsewhere.

### BIJOUTERIE EL-YASMINE *Jewellery*
**68 Rue Riad Zitoun el-Jedid; ⏰ 10am-7pm**
Yasmin's simplified takes on traditional motifs look (and cost) like adornments instead of dowry payments. Check out hammered silver teaspoons with striped ebony and enamel handles, lucky turquoise enamel hand of Fatima earrings, and Tuareg-inspired cocktail rings that look like hypnotist's props >

NEIGHBOURHOODS

RIADS ZITOUN & KASBAH

with concentric circles in dark wood and bright orange enamel.

### 🏠 COULEURS ORIENTALES MARRAKESH
*Accessories & Moroccan Crafts*

☎ 024 398739; 233 Rue Riad Zitoun el-Jedid; ⏰ 10am-7pm

Your one-stop shop for snazzy Marrakesh mementos, including clever tasselled silk necklaces, striped silk flip-flops, and Tigmi cooperative placemats in deep orange with an embroidered zigzag edge. The fixed prices are less than what you'd pay for similar items along Rue de la Liberté (see p42).

### 🏠 CREATIONS PNEUMATIQUES
*Homewares & Moroccan Crafts*

☎ 066 091746; 110-111 Rue Riad Zitoun el-Kedim; ⏰ 7am-10pm

Atlas Abdelghani is a Bob Marley fan, as you can see from the posters he's framed with recycled tyres, with one word embedded over Marley's head: 'Michelin'. This is one recycling *maâlem* with a sneaky sense of humour and serious ingenuity; crafts range from treasure chests with air valves as drawer pulls to tyre-tread flip-flops with serious traction.

### 🏠 GNAOUA MUSIC SHOP
*Musical Instruments*

84 Rue Riad Zitoun el-Jedid; ⏰ 10am-8pm

You'll have to duck to avoid banging the drums over the doorway with your head, but you've come to the right place to go Gnaoua and join a jam session. These are the handmade, rustic instruments played in the Djemaa el-Fna, from recycled-metal castanets to goatskins stretched over sturdy frames that can take a real pounding.

### 🏠 GRAND BIJOUTERIE
*Jewellery*

Rue Bab Mellah, opposite entrance to Bahia Palace; ⏰ 9.30am-8pm

Get reeled in by small silver charms, and hooked by gold chandelier earrings that tickle shoulders and deplete bank reserves. Pieces are sold by weight, so serious shoppers should know the going market rate for gold and silver and mind the scales. The fancy filigree jewellery hails from India, but you'll still spy some local jewellers diligently plying their trade.

### 🏠 JAMADE
*Homewares & Moroccan Crafts*

☎ 024 429042; 1 Place Douar Graoua, off Rue Riad Zitoun el-Jedid; ⏰ 10am-1.30pm & 3.30-7.30pm

As you might guess from Jamade's deep-purple floor and space-age orange ceramic tea sets, this is not your granny's idea of a Moroccan crafts shop.

## MY, AREN'T YOU THOUGHTFUL

By bringing these Marrakshi treats to friends back home, you're also promoting fair trade, worthy causes and recycling in Marrakesh:

> Fashion and hand-carved thuya wood boxes from Cooperative Artisanale Femmes de Marrakech (p84)
> Argan oil from Assouss Cooperative D'Argane (p99)
> Tigmi embroidered coasters from Jamade (opposite) and Tigmi tasselled placemats from Couleurs Orientales Marrakesh (opposite)
> Linens embroidered with lucky Berber motifs at Association Al Kawtar (p92), a nonprofit centre for disabled women
> Recycled tyre crafts from Creations Pneumatiques (opposite) and sardine-tin home décor from Kifkif (p100)

The stock is stylish and prices are fixed; featured local designers include Tigmi, the women's cooperative that embroiders coasters with striking symbols to bring Berber *baraka* (good vibes) to your coffee table.

### 🖼 MADEMOISELLE IBTISSAM'S ORIGINAL DESIGN *Homewares*

☎ 024 380361; www.original-design
-mrk.com; 47 Place des Ferblantiers,
near Badi Palace; 🕑 9.30am-12.30pm &
2.30-7.30pm
With handcrafted table accessories this glamorous, you could order takeaway and still wow your guests: rocket ship–red tagine presentation dishes, linen tablecloths with playful pompoms, twin mini-tagines for salt and pepper, tasselled silk napkin holders and more. The fixed prices are already a bargain.

### 🖼 MELLAH MARKET
*Food Market*

**Ave Houmane el-Fetouaki, near Place des Ferblantiers;** 🕑 8am-1pm & 3-7pm
For the south side of the city, this is a major source for food, flowers and other household goods. Fair warning to vegetarians: the door closest to Place des Ferblantiers leads directly to the chicken and meat area.

### 🖼 MOUHASSIN EPICES *Spices*

**10 Rue de la Bahia;** 🕑 9am-noon &
3-7pm
Take home your own Moroccan culinary and cosmetic secrets from this sweet, straight-dealing merchant of spices and natural remedies. Mouhassin sells good-quality saffron, ras al-hanout spice mix, amber perfume, rosewater and more at reasonable prices – shop here first before you get rooked in the Rahba Kedima.

### WARDA LA MOUCHE
*Fashion*

☎ 067 347374; 1 Derb Sidi Boulafdaiel; ⏰ 9.30am-9pm Tue-Sun

This local designer makes glamour look easy with embroidered tunic T-shirts, metal-embroidered kaftans and psychedelic slippers. Prices are fixed, and about what you'd pay for mass-produced basics back home.

# EAT

### LA SULTANA
*French–Moroccan*                                $$$

☎ 024 388008; www.lasultanamarra kech.com; Rue de la Kasbah

So this is what it means to be spoiled for choice. Do you dine in the intimate cloisters, or on the roof overlooking the Saadian Tombs? Would you prefer the French duck that's more tender than your last love affair, or the Moroccan *bastilla* (pigeon pie) so light it could blow away in strong breezes? Prices are high and service is slow, but the food and setting are sublime.

### NID' CIGOGNE
*Sandwiches & Snacks*                             $

☎ 024 382092; 60 Place des Tombeaux Saadians; ⏰ 9am-9pm

This rooftop restaurant lets you get up close and personal with the storks across the way at the Saadian Tombs, and offers service-able grilled *kefta* (spiced meatball) sandwiches and light salads, and nothing-special tagines. Service is slow, but pleasant considering those steep stairs.

### RESTAURANT PLACE DES FERBLANTIERS
*Moroccan Á La Carte*                             $

**West entrance Place des Ferblantiers, near Mellah Market**

For a quick, tasty tagine served bubbling hot right off the burner, look no more at touristy palace restaurants with plodding service. Plop down on a plastic chair in the courtyard, and have whatever's freshest that day – the meat and produce come from the Mellah Market across the street, and you can see the cook whipping up tagines right in front of you.

### RYAD JANA
*Moroccan Á La Carte*                             $

☎ 024 429872; 149 Toualat Kennaria

Finally, a family-run riad restaurant that serves á la carte lunches at realistic prices, along with generous helpings of Moroccan hospitality. Enjoy your lamb tagine with prunes and almonds in the restful garden for only slightly more than you'd pay to dine on a skimpy version in the dusty Djemaa, and win huge accolades for trying even a few words of Moroccan Arabic.

## TANGIA
*Moroccan Á La Carte* $$
☎ 024 383836; 14 Derb Jedid, Mellah;
⏲ 8am-1am

Can a standard chicken tagine with olives and preserved lemons really be worth almost three times what you'd pay in the Djemaa? Tangia will quell any such doubt with aromatic herbed olives, caramelised sauce with a lemony tang but no bitterness, and plump chicken very different from the anorexic variety served elsewhere – and at the next table over, the editors of American and French *Vogue* also seemed to approve. The namesake lamb stew may be hit or miss, but this is fancy-tagine heaven.

## DRINK
### KOSYBAR *Bar*
☎ 024 380324; 47 Place des Ferblantiers;
⏲ 6pm-5am;

The Marrakesh-meets-Kyoto interiors are plenty fabulous, with 19th-century *zellij* bumping up against Shinto-shrine exposed beams, but you'd be wise to skip the less-than-inspired sushi and head straight up to the roof terrace bar overlooking the Badi Palace. Here Moroccan wines are served with a side of samba, and storks give you the once-over from nearby nests.

## PLAY

### DAR ES-SALAM *Cabaret*
☎ 024 443520; www.daressalam.com;
170 Rue Riad Zitoun el-Kedim; ⏲ 7-11pm

This restaurant was featured in Hitchcock's *The Man Who Knew Too Much*, and it still specialises in surprise endings. The unexpected twist comes around 9pm, when a woman in a spangled unitard emerges bearing a tray of lit candles on her head and proceeds to perform callisthenic dance manoeuvres like a pyromaniac Romanian gymnast. But the night will not be over until the final twist – the Berber band breaks into a rousing bar-mitzvah chorus of 'Hava Nagila'.

### LES BAINS DE MARRAKESH
*Hammam*
☎ 024 381428; www.lesbainsdemarra kech.com; 2 Derb Serdra, near Bab er-Rob

The most romantic spa in town, if you have a special other, Les Bains will treat the two of you to a private hammam (Dh80 each) and a candlelit rose-petal bath in side-by-side purple *tadelakt* (polished plaster) tubs (Dh150 each). Special treatments range from masks of crushed local herbs (Dh100 including hammam) to *gommage* (body scrub) with desert sand and essential oils (Dh180). Bookings are required.

### ⚜ SULTANA SPA *Hammam*

☎ 024 388008; www.lasultanamarra
kech.com; Rue de la Kasbah, next to
Saadian Tombs; Ⓟ

Through the majestic archways
lies this glistening marble spa, its
glowing emerald pool flanked by
private cabins for gentle *gommage*
treatments with organic plant ex-
tracts and essential oils (€25). Get
the royal treatment with two- or
four-handed amber-oil massages
(two-handed €45 per 50 minutes,
four-handed €50 per 30 minutes)
in a roof-terrace pavilion.

Drift off on a boat-bed at Riad Enija (p128)

# RIADS

Paris has its cathedrals, New York its skyscrapers, but riads are what set Marrakesh apart. These spectacular mud-brick courtyard mansions are oases of calm in the bustling Medina: push through the brass-studded wooden doors and suddenly you're in a courtyard lined with soaring Moorish arches and cozy *bhous* (seating nooks). Metre-thick mud-brick walls block out street noise, so that when the door closes on the hubbub of the souqs you can hear burbling courtyard fountains and songbirds in pomegranate trees. Behind its pink walls Marrakesh has more authentic riads than any other city in North Africa, and they include exuberantly ornamented examples from the 17th century.

Over the past decade, hundreds of these historic family homes have been sold and reinvented as guesthouses, mainly by Europeans. The best are not just marvels of the Marrakshi tradition of craftsmanship – which guesthouses helped revive – but unforgettable experiences of Marrakshi hospitality, complete with insights into the local culture and shifting social mores. 'Riad' is now a synonym for guesthouse, and the ones highlighted in this chapter offer a range of must-have Marrakshi experiences: made-to-order Moroccan feasts from an ingenious *dada* (cook); hammam treatments; courses on everything from cooking to mosaics taught by a *maâlem* (expert craftsperson); and excursions to mountain villages and the Sahara beyond. Staying in a riad isn't just about sleeping in posh digs; it's about gaining an understanding of Marrakesh behind those studded doors. For information on accommodation outside the Medina, see p132.

## RIADS

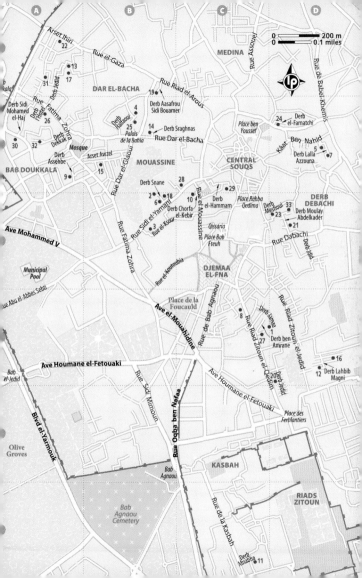

**A**

**B**

**C**

**D**

22 Arset Ihiri

Rue el-Gaza

13
17
31

Rue Jedid

Derb Jedid

Rue Fatima Zohra

Rue Ihihi

DAR EL-BACHA

19 Rue Riad el-Arous

Rue Assouel

Rue de Bab el-Khemis

Derb Sidi Mohamed el-Haj

26

Derb Aasafrou Sidi Bouamer

24 Derb el-Farnatchi

Derb Halnaui

4

Derb Dekkak R

Derb Sraghnas

Kaat Ben Nahid

30
32

Mosque

25 Palais de la Bahia

14 Rue Dar el-Bacha

Place ben Youssef

Derb Lalla Azzouna
5
7

Derb Assehbe

Arset Awzel

MOUASSINE

CENTRAL SOUQS

9

15

Derb Snane

28

Rue Dar el-Glaoui

2
18

10

Rue Sidi el-Yamani

29

Place Rahba Qedima

DERB DEBACHI

Derb el-Hammam

Derb Menhoui
33
23

Derb Moulay Abdelkader

Rue el-Ksour

Derb Chorfa el-Kebir

Rue el-Mouassine

21

Rue Dabachi

Qissaria

Rue Fatima Zohra

Place Bab Fteuh

Derb Jdid

Rue el-Koutoubia

DJEMAA EL-FNA

Ave Mohammed V

Municipal Pool

Place de la Foucauld

Rue Abu el-Abbes Sebti

Ave el-Mouahidine

Rue de Bab Agnaou

8

Derb Jamaa

Derb Riad Zitoun el-Jedid

27
1

Derb ben Amrane

Ave Houmane el-Fetouaki

Rue Riad Zitoun el-Qedim

16

12 Derb Lahbib Magni

Rue Sidi Mimoun

Bab el-Jedid

Ave Houmane el-Fetouaki

Derb Jedid

20

Blvd el-Yarmouk

Place des Ferblantiers

Rue Oqba ben Nafaa

Bab Agnaou

Olive Groves

KASBAH

Bab Agnaou Cemetery

Rue de la Kasbah

RIADS ZITOUN

Derb Mnabha
11

0      200 m
0      0.1 miles

## RIAD RATES

Rates can vary dramatically depending on the time of year and length of stay – inquire about specials for longer stays and low-season rates via the various riads' websites. Low season is usually summer (mid-June to August) and winter (mid-January to mid-March). Book a month ahead and expect high-season rates during major European holidays (especially Christmas/New Year and Easter/Passover). Mid-season rates cover most of spring and autumn, and are indicated in this chapter as follows, including breakfast:

> $$$ Top End: over Dh1100
> $$ Midrange: Dh750 to Dh1100
> $ Budget: under Dh750

# MOUASSINE

### DAR AL KOUNOUZ                                $$
☎ 024 390773; www.daralkounouz
.com; 54 Derb Snane; ✖ ☐ ♣
The roof terrace overlooks the royal Dar el-Bacha next door, but the real action is downstairs, where you can learn the chef's secrets in the kitchen or be massaged in the marble hammam. Lazy mornings are meant for curling up by the fireplace in the library under the stained-glass cupola. Babysitting available.

### DAR ATTAJMIL                                $$
☎ 024 426966; www.darattajmil.com;
23 Rue el-ksour; ✖ ☐ ☎
This riad is rosy and relaxed, and you will be too after a few days within these Marrakshi pink *tadelakt* (polished plaster) walls. Lucrezia and her attentive staff offer a warm welcome and an even warmer rooftop hammam,

plus scrumptious Moroccan-fusion dinners, cooking classes, *zellij* (mosaic) workshops and Essaouira escapes. Wi-fi available.

### DAR MOUASSINE                                $$
☎ 024 445287; www.darmouassine
.com; 148 Derb Snane; ✖ ☐ ☎
Skip the guitar lessons: against this glam backdrop of mod furnishings, ironwork balconies and original 17th-century doors, anyone looks like a rock star. Stage album cover shoots beside the *tadelakt* pool or in the Jacuzzi, and live large in the Cardamom Suite with its intricate woodwork ceiling and turreted bathroom. Wi-fi available.

## TOP FIVE FOR FOOD
> Dar Attajmil (left)
> Maison Mnabha (p122)
> Riad 72 (p117)
> La Maison Arabe (p124)
> Casa Lalla (p122)

## LES JARDINS DE MOUASSINE $

☎ 72 581078; www.lesjardinsdemouas
sine.com; 20 Derb Chorfa el-Kebir;

Recover from shopping fatigue and forget you're steps away from Medina souqs in the in-house hammam or library, or on sunny terraces across three interconnected riads. The standard rooms are more pleasant than the knick-knack-cluttered suites, so save your cash for trips to the mountains or coast…or more shopping.

## RIAD AUGGY $$

☎ 024 440694; www.riadauggy.com; 129 Derb Snane;

A setting for high-society intrigue, in handsomely appointed guest rooms with hand-painted wood-work and lordly wrought-iron beds. Embarrassingly generous breakfasts are served in the patio courtyard under the banana tree or atop the breezy roof terrace.

## RIAD L'ORANGERAIE $$$

☎ 61 238789; www.riadorangeraie.com; 61 Rue Sidi el-Yamani;

It's smooth and suave, with per-fectly buffed *tadelakt* walls, mas-saging showers (the best in town), a generous pool and sprawling rooms. This place has all the right moves, with five employees look-ing after seven rooms, a car and driver at your disposal, excellent

Rock star style: Cardamom Suite at Dar Mouassine

breakfasts and soothing hammam treatments. Wi-fi available.

## RIAD MAGELLAN $$

☎ 024 376070; www.riadmagellan.com; 62 Derb el-Hammam;

World travellers will want to put down roots in this retro riad, where steamer trunks, antique globes and 1930s fans bring back the cosmopolitan glamour of Art Deco Marrakesh. A terrace hot tub and deep-tissue massages soothe away economy-airfare kinks, and kindly staff make this well-hidden but ideally located retreat feel like home.

# RIADS ZITOUN & KASBAH

## CASA LALLA $$

☎ 024 429757; www.casalalla.com; 16 Derb Jamaa;

Recipe for a delectable riad: take central location on hidden alley, add in-house hammam and Jacuzzi, and stir with inventive market menu served nightly by French chef. Finish with restrained décor in shades of salt and pepper with dashes of harissa (chilli), and garnish guestrooms with sleeping lofts and fireplaces.

## JNANE MOGADOR $

☎ 024 426324; www.jnanemogador .com; 116 Rue Riad Zitoun el-Qedim;

The sweetest deal in the souqs: a prime location, in-house hammam, double-decker roof terraces, and owner Mohammed's laid-back hospitality. A favourite with diplomats and artists; book ahead and enjoy fascinating breakfast conversation.

## MAISON MNABHA $$

☎ 024 381325; www.maisonmnabha .com; 32-3 Derb Mnabha, Kasbah;

Treasure-hunters seek out this 17th-century Kasbah hideaway brimming with elusive finds. In antique-filled salons celebrity chefs, famous authors and other regulars mingle over Khadija's seasonal cuisine. English brothers Peter and Lawrence and manager Aziz are a

Don't miss dinnertime at Maison Mnabha

## TOP FIVE FOR AUTHENTIC MOROCCAN HOSPITALITY

> Dar Tayib (p127)
> Marhbabikoum (below)
> Riad Akka (below)
> Jnane Mogador (opposite)
> Riad Kniza (p126)

wealth of impartial antiques advice and cultural insight – Peter holds a PhD in Kasbah history – and arrange restorative massages, henna tattooing and eco-conscious desert adventures.

### MARHBABIKOUM                    $

☎ 024 375204; www.marhbabikoum.com; 43 Derb Lahbib Magni; ▢ 🔀 🚹
The name means welcome, and you'll feel it when you step through the door. Khalil and Véronique run their mellow riad family-style, so you're automatically invited for tea, chats, card games and Moroccan jam sessions already in progress. If you can tear yourself away, mountain excursions can be arranged.

### RIAD AKKA                    $$$

☎ 024 375767; www.riad-akka.com; 65 Derb Lahbib Magni; 🔀 ▢ 🖥
A total sweetheart of a riad: gorgeous and genuinely kind to you. With Arabic sayings about cross-cultural understanding painted around the patio, the décor is strikingly modern and upbeat – and the same can be said about the staff. Trust manager Mbarka for restaurant and shopping recommendations, and splash out for the in-house hammam and graphite-*tadelakt* Taroudant and Tafraout rooms.

### RIAD EDEN                    $

☎ 072 046910; www.riadeden-marrakech.com; 25 Derb Jedid; 🔀 ▢ 🚹
Generous cooks, a comfy living room and energetic young French family owners make the Eden a sociable spot. Pull up a chair in the kitchen and watch culinary magic happen. Standard rooms are more snug and sweet than the suites, especially the African-inspired Fig room and the rooftop Orange room.

### RIAD LES BOUGAINVILLIERS                    $$$

☎ 024 391717; www.riadlesbougainvilliers.com; 5 Derb Ben Amrane; 🔀 🖥 🚹
Like Prozac, this sunny double riad lifts moods overnight, with soaring archways, exposed brick and natural wood. Suites verge on bland, but junior suite Jasmin and double Jacaranda induce instant harmony. Staff is professional without being stuffy, and arrange arrivals by horse-drawn carriage, massages, babysitting, mountain

excursions, cooking classes and weddings.

# BAB DOUKKALA & DAR EL-BACHA

## DAR BARAKA & DAR KARAM $

☎ 024 391609; www.marrakech-riads
.net; 18 &11 Derb Halfaoui; 🏠

High style at low prices, with sharp staff and tranquil, mostly white décor focusing attention on authentic period details: arabesque archways, cedar ceilings and polychrome stucco. These conjoined-twin riads are connected by a vast roof terrace, plus a shared fondness for rose petals, lanterns and firm beds.

## LA MAISON ARABE $$$

☎ 024 387010; www.lamaisonarabe
.com; 1 Derb Assehbe; 🏠 🖥 🏠

The legendary restaurant is now a glamorous guesthouse, tastefully outfitted with North African antiques, a yummy restaurant, slinky bar, acclaimed culinary classes and a scrumptious hammam where

> **TOP FIVE FOR CULTURAL EXPERIENCE**
> > Riad al Massarah (opposite)
> > Riad Sahara Nour (p127)
> > Riyad el Cadi (p129)
> > Riad Bledna (p133)
> > Jnane Tamsna (p133)

you can marinate in baths of local herbs and mineral salts.

## NOIR D'IVOIRE $$$

☎ 024 380975; www.noir-d-ivoire.com;
31 Derb Jedid; 🏠 🖥 🏠

The gobsmacking opulence includes a foyer chandelier 4.5m wide and guest mobile phones supplied by English owner/tastemaker Jill Fechtmann. Sink into soft armchairs in the well-stocked library, lounge by the grand piano in the leather-clad cocktail bar, and enjoy shiatsu and chocolates by the private spa fireplace. Decadent, but thoughtful too, from the water-conserving filtered pool to organic spa products.

## RIAD 12 $$

☎ 024 387629; www.riad12.com; 12
Derb Sraghnas; 🏠 🏠

The heart-stealing younger sister of 72, with a sunnier disposition, magazine-ready looks, and echoing rooms that would qualify as suites elsewhere. The downside: you'll have to be pried from your butterfly chair by the courtyard pool to take advantage of the excellent meals and hammam at Riad 72.

## RIAD 72 $$$

☎ 024 387629; www.riad72.com; 72
Arset Awzel; 🏠 🏠

Like a kaftan-clad supermodel on a Vespa, the 72 defines jet-set chic. All rooms feature snappy amenities such as Pop Art pillows, bathrobes and almond cologne, and the hammam, cupola-topped Karma suite and yoga classes get guests catwalk-ready. But even supermodels couldn't resist Fatima's lamb melting into roast quince and other seasonal treats, served atop the tallest roof terrace around.

Michael redesigned this ancient riad to maximise comfort and sunlight, and minimise electrical and water use and eco-impact. Offers top-notch hammam, massages, cooking lessons, and eco-friendly excursions – all while donating to local nonprofits, providing full benefits to a staff of five, and heading local recycling initiatives.

### RIAD AL MASSARAH   $$$
☎ 024 383206; www.riadalmassarah .com; 26 Derb Jedid; ⛶ 💻 📠
The ultimate feel-good hideaway: British-French owners Michel and

### RIAD BELBARAKA   $$
☎ 061 306591; www.maisonbelbaraka .com; 242 Derb Aasafrou Sidi Bouamer; ⛶
Buddha presides over the entry, a Portuguese documentary is filmed

Tranquility at Riad Belbaraka

in the foyer, and Greek-Moroccan owners Charlotte and Rachid bring mint tea to sunbathing Scandinavians: just another charmed day at this multiculti riad. The pick of kitschy-cute rooms is Pigeonnier, whose aviary-niche shower inspires nesting instincts. Staff arrange massages, henna tattoos and public hammam trips.

### RIAD EL-SAGAYA $

☎ 024 380353; www.riad-elsagaya .com; 150 Arset Ihiri;

London law-firm escapee Annabella and her husband Youssef offer laid-back hospitality and nine cheerful, shabby-chic guestrooms with *tadelakt* bathrooms. Staff organise babysitting plus loads of activities, from *tadelakt* workshops with a master artisan and henna tattooing lessons to accompanied public hammam trips and eco-friendly mountain treks.

### RIAD JULIA $

☎ 024 376022; www.riadjulia.com; 14 Derb Halfaoui;

How clever – each room highlights a Marrakesh handicraft, from mother-of-pearl inlay to chip-carved cedar wood. Five of the seven rooms have air conditioning, and all are well-kept and comfy, including bathrobes and soft Berber wedding blankets with coin fringes for good luck (wink,

wink). English-speaking Ziad arranges excursions, henna tattooing and dinners under the Berber roof tent. Babysitting available.

### RIAD KNIZA $$$

☎ 024 376942; www.riadkniza.com; 34 Derb L'Hotel;

Gregarious grandeur in an 18th-century mansion restored by antiques aficionado Mohammed Bouskri. In cushy salons and on sunny patios, people mingle easily, staff take the time to chat, and drinks are constantly refreshed. Learn to make signature lamb and chicken dishes, soak in the new spa or be whisked off to Palmeraie camel or horseback rides by English-speaking chauffeurs. Babysitting is available and there's wi-fi internet access.

### RIAD NEJMA LOUNGE $

☎ 024 382341; www.riad-nejmalounge .com; 45 Derb Sidi Mohamed el-Haj;

Surprise: the hippest riad in town is among the most affordable. Pierre and Alex play up the mod, organic appeal of their riad with splashes of colour: a chocolate brown wall in one guestroom, a pink chaise longue in another, and a roof terrace bright red as a sunburn. It's handy to Nouvelle Ville restaurants and shops, but don't miss the tasty meals here or the in-house boutique.

## RIAD SABLES CHAUD $$

☎ 024 383142; www.riadsablechaud
-marrakech.com; 135 Derb Jedid; ⚅ ⚉

A live-in literary salon, with 1930s
leather club chairs and modern-
ist sculpture that make you look
clever by association. French jour-
nalist resident-owner Françoise
hosts memorable meals with her
translator/chef, formerly of Dar
Moha (p93). Board games, bikes,
books and DVDs are at guests'
disposal, and cooking classes,
massages and Berber village dining excursions possible.

## RIAD SAHARA NOUR $$

☎ 024 376570; www.riadsaharanour
-marrakech.com; 118 Derb Dekkak

Learn something new every day at
this artistically inclined guesthouse,
where you can roll out of bed and
into a class on Middle Eastern
dance or Moroccan calligraphy.
Classes are open to nonguests
and subject to separate booking,
so reserve early and ask about
English-speaking instructors.

# CENTRAL SOUQS & DERB DEBACHI

## DAR HANANE $$

☎ 024 377737; www.dar-hanane.com; 9
Derb Lalla Azzouna; ⚅ ⚏ ⚉

Lolling comes easily with high-
thread-count linens, iPod docking
stations and soothing, minimalist

décor. The loft living room features
an honesty bar where you track
your Bonassia Cabernet intake
(ahem). Chef Aisha's flair for French
and Moroccan specialities makes
restaurant trips unnecessary, but
English-speaking staff organises
excursions for the restless.

## DAR TAYIB $

☎ 024 383010; www.riad-dartayib.com;
19 Derb Lalla Azzouna; ⚅ ⚏

Other riads have glamour, but this
place has *baraka* (good vibes).
Marrakshi Latifa and French architect husband Vincent bring on the
Berber charm, from good-luck-
symbol carpets to winking tinwork
lamps. The Yasmina room beats
love potions with a canopy bed,
tub and mood lighting, and clever
rooftop hideaways end writer's
block. Vincent leads excursions,
and Latifa organises dinners and
cooking classes.

## RIAD EL BORJ $$

☎ 024 391223; www.riadelborj.com; 63
Derb Moulay Adbelkader; ⚅ ⚏ ⚉ ⚏

This was once Grand-Vizier
Madani Glaoui's lookout, and

RIADS

## BEYOND LOOKS: CHOOSING YOUR RIAD

On the web you'll find hundreds of riads in Marrakesh that appear picture-perfect, candlelit and strewn with rose petals. But some lovely riads aren't licensed, which means you have no guarantees of upkeep, hygiene and decent workplace conditions, where workers get at least the US$0.50/hour minimum wage and time off. Some 200 unlicensed riads were summarily closed by the government in spring 2003, leaving travellers stranded without accommodation in high season.

The licensed riads in this chapter have been selected not on looks alone, but for convenient locations, helpful staff, home-cooked Moroccan meals and must-have Marrakshi experiences such as cooking courses, mountain excursions and hammams. Lonely Planet recommends riads that promote environmentally sustainable practices, fair compensation, time off for employees, cultural exchange and genuine Moroccan hospitality. You can help: give riad feedback at www.lonelyplanet.com/contact.

now you too can lord it over the neighbours in the suite with original *zellij*, double-height ceilings and skylit tub. Or try the tower hideaway with the rippled ceiling and book nook. Loaf by the pool in the 'Berber annex', let off steam in the hammam, or take advantage of mountain excursions and babysitting.

### RIAD ENIJA $$$
☎ 024 440926; www.riadenija.com; 9 Derb Mesfioui; ⬛ ▢ ▣
Live a charmed existence next door to Rahba Kedima magic sellers at the exquisite Enija. Brushing up against the 280-year-old architecture are modern design showpieces, rare plants, turtles and supermodels. Drift off on a boat in the Anenome Room or a royal Egyptian barque in the Pourpre Room; awake for brunch

in the garden and indulge in facials from the in-house beautician and dips in the new pool. Wi-fi available.

### RIAD FARNATCHI $$$
☎ 024 384910; www.riadfarnatchi.com; 2 Derb el-Farnatchi; ⬛ ▢ ▣
Getting used to this treatment could be dangerous. Nine suites aim to please, with skylights and fireplaces shedding flattering glows on private salons, fossil bathtubs appeasing the travel-weary, and sumptuous suede coverlets begging a snuggle. You simply have to lick your lips and admire a *djellaba* (robe) and abracadabra, Canadian director Lynn Perez and her expert staff appear with fresh watermelon-mint juice and a tailor. Wi-fi internet, chauffeured cars, personal shoppers, hammam, massages…the works.

## RIYAD EL CADI $$$

☎ 024 378655; www.riyadelcadi.com;
87 Derb Moulay Abdelkader; ✂ ▢ ▣

A Medina within the Medina, this labyrinth of five riads offers unexpected delights at every turn: lovers' balconies, secret alcoves, a Marrakshi red hammam and glimpses of an outstanding collection of rare Berber textiles. A staff of 15 keeps occupants happy in 12 pristine rooms and suites, ranging from the mod black-and-white double Aleppo to the elegant two-bedroom Douiriya junior suite.

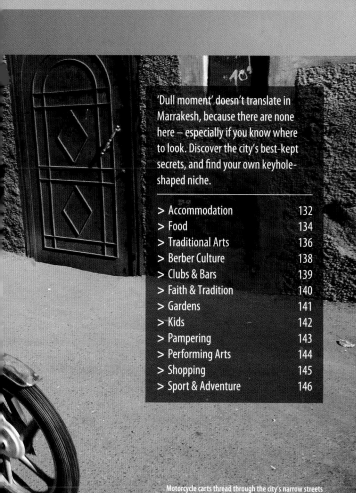

'Dull moment' doesn't translate in Marrakesh, because there are none here – especially if you know where to look. Discover the city's best-kept secrets, and find your own keyhole-shaped niche.

Motorcycle carts thread through the city's narrow streets

# ACCOMMODATION

'Are you happy? Everything's good? How about your family?' What could be the start of a therapy session elsewhere is a greeting in Marrakesh – hospitality has been practised and perfected for a millennium at this trading post. Courtyard fountains are elegantly strewn with rose petals, mint tea is poured from on high without splashing and cosy *bhous* (seating nooks) invite conversation. Riads (courtyard mansions) offer Marrakshi hospitality at its most idyllic; see p117 for listings. For the best riad rates, go for three days or more in low season, or email through their websites to ask if you can be accommodated in your price range and dates.

The personal attention of a riad can't be matched by a 100-room resort, but Marrakesh's best hotels offer convenience and consistency, and in high season (p120) may be your only choice. The swankiest are in the Hivernage, including historic **Mamounia** (www.mamounia.com). The best value are in downtown Guéliz amid boutiques, galleries and local-favourite restaurants: **Oudaya** (www.oudaya.ma), **Hôtel du Pacha** ( ☎ 024 431326), **Caspien** (www.lecaspien-hotel.com), **Toulousain** (www.geocities.com/hotel_toulousain) and the pleasant, train-station-handy **Meryem** (www.hotelmeryem-marrakech.com).

When choosing a location in the Medina, follow your bliss. Budget hotels cluster around the Djemaa el-Fna, ranging from cheerfully well travelled to woefully world-weary. Central Mouassine has the most historic homes hidden amid souqs and mosques – bring earplugs to muffle 5am calls to prayer. Palaces and museums cluster in the Riads Zitoun and royal Kasbah, and main streets from the Djemaa el-Fna to the Bahia Palace are lined with artisans. You'll be taking more taxis if you stay in the Kasbah but you'll get more glimpses of authentic Marrakshi neighbourhood life.

Though Derb Debachi is next to bustling Djemaa and Rahba Qedima, its hushed backstreets seem a world apart. Bab Doukkala is convenient to the Nouvelle Ville, and this medieval maze has its own food souqs, boutiques, hammams and upmarket restaurants.

Villas in the Palmeraie let you chill out in a palm oasis. **Les Deux Tours** (www.les-deuxtours.com) is splendid modern-Moroccan and it kicked off the Palmeraie trend; **Dar Ayniwen** (www.dar-ayniwen.com) is a family-run eclectic retreat (check out the champagne buckets). Most Palmeraie guesthouses feature pools, hammams, gardens and lounge bars – **Jnane Tamsna** (www .jnanetamsna.com) and **Bled al-Fassia** (www.bledalfassia.com) offer organic cooking courses, while **Riad Bledna** (www.riadbledna.com) offers a range of arts courses including weaving, *tadelakt* (polished plaster), *zellij* (mosaic) and *zellij* patchwork quilting (see boxed text, p66). Environmentally savvy golfers will check into **La Pause** (www.lapause-marrakech.com), an Agafay Desert oasis 30 minutes away with its sod-free, all-terrain course for golf and disc golf.

Last-minute and package deals are listed on Marrakesh's main accommodation websites: www.ilove-marrakech.com, www.maroc-selection .com, www.terremaroc.com and www.riadsmorocco.com. Many riads and villas can be rented by the week: check listings on www.marrakech-riads .net, www.marrakech-medina.com and www.habibihomes.com.

## BEST UNDER DH500

> Riad Eden (www.riadeden-marrakech .com)
> Riad Julia (www.riadjulia.com)
> Riad Nejma Lounge (www.riad -nejmalounge.com)
> Hôtel Gallia ( ☎ 024 445913)
> Jnane Mogador (www.jnanemogador .com)

## BEST FOR ROMANCE

> Dar Tayib (p127)
> Riyad el Cadi (p129)
> La Sultana (www.lasultanamarrakech .com)
> Dar Attajmil (p120)
> Riad Enija (p128)

## BEST OFF THE BEATEN PATH

> La Pause (www.lapause-marrakech .com)
> Riad Akka (p123)
> Maison Mnabha (p122)
> Riad al Massarah (p125)
> Riad Magellan (p121)

## BEST PALMERAIE ESCAPES

> Jnane Tamsna (www.jnanetamsna .com)
> Les Deux Tours (www.les-deuxtours .com)
> Dar Ayniwen (www.dar-ayniwen.com)
> Riad Bledna (www.riadbledna.com)
> Villa Maha (www.villa-maha.com)

# FOOD

Even atheists find foodie religion in Marrakesh, where the dishes keep coming until you protest *'Alhamdullilah'*, or 'Praise be to God'. Breakfast on *beghrir,* pancakes with a spongy crumpet texture drizzled with cactus flower honey; lavishly lunch on *mechoui,* slow-roasted almond-stuffed lamb served with cumin, olives and *khoobz* (bread); and after several laps of the souqs, you'll muster appetite for a savoury, seasonal tagine (clay-pot stew) in the Djemaa el-Fna. Few things make Marrakshis happier than to see guests eat with gusto, so go on, do your part for international relations and have dessert. Leave room for *kaab el-ghazal* (crescent-shaped 'gazelle's horn' cookies stuffed with almond paste and laced with orange-flower water) or dessert *bastilla* (layers of flaky pastry with cream and toasted nuts).

In the Nouvelle Ville, you can join Marrakesh's rising middle class for pizza at Catanzaro (p50) and Niagara (p52) or barbecue at sidewalk restaurants along Rue ibn Aicha. Fashionable Marrakshis prefer restaurants that do double duty as discos (see p139). Alcohol is now served in many, but not all, restaurants; see individual reviews for details.

For superb home-style cooking, try a riad, where meals are made to order by the in-house *dada* (cook). Adventurous eaters tuck into steaming bowls of snails or sheep's-head stew at thronged stalls in the Djemaa el-Fna (p72) or Ben Youssef Food Stall Qissaria (p86).

For a big night out, Marrakesh has some fantastic Moroccan, Mediterranean and fusion restaurants – but also many tourist-trap 'palace restaurants'. If your footsteps echo, your waiter is sheepishly costumed like Aladdin and there's a stage set up for a laser-light show, don't expect authentic cuisine. Hold out for a proper *diffa* (feast; see p21) at the places recommended below, and a heartfelt '*Alhamdullilah*'.

### BEST INVENTIVE MOROCCAN

> Dar Moha (p93)
> Villa Flore (p103)
> Patisserie al-Jawda (p53)
> Le Foundouk (p87)
> Riad 72 (p94)

### BEST TRADITIONAL MOROCCAN

> Al Fassia (p47)
> Tangia (p115)
> La Maison Arabe Restaurant (p94)
> Tobsil (p103)
> Chez Chegrouni (p71)

### BEST STREET EATS

> Mechoui Alley (p74)
> Ben Youssef Food Stall Qissaria (p86)
> Plats Haj Boujemaa (p53) and other grill restaurants on Rue ibn Aicha
> Djemaa el-Fna food stalls (p72)
> Samak al Bahria (p53)

### BEST BREAKS FROM MOROCCAN

> Beyrouth (p48)
> Catanzaro (p50)
> Le Chat Qui Rit (p51)
> La Table du Marché (p50)
> Le Grand Café de la Poste (p52)

**Top left** Meat-lovers' paradise: Mechoui Alley (p74) **Above** Service with a smile: Souq Ablueh (p81)

# TRADITIONAL ARTS

When a twinkling lamp or scarlet handbag catches your eye in the souqs, look around and you might find the *maâlem* (master craftsperson) nearby, already at work on another fabulous creation. This is your chance to extend your compliments, see how it's made, maybe even try your hand at a traditional Moroccan craft – just don't be dismayed if you're not a natural. Marrakshi *maâlems* make their handiwork look easy, but it takes years of apprenticeship and skills handed down through generations to master those medieval tools and time-honoured techniques. A *zellij* apprentice can take months to master just one of the 400-plus essential shapes in *zellij* patterns, and mathematicians have only recently begun to understand the variation-within-repetition 'Penrose patterns' found within Islamic mosaic motifs.

Hot spots to watch *maâlems* work wonders are the north end of the souqs and the Ensemble Artisanal (p40). You often get the best deals on handcrafted goods straight from the maker, but really, in a world of mass-produced, machine-made goods, these labour-intensive crafts are a bargain at any price. Back home, you can't exactly nip round to your local *tadelakt* artisan for a silky, hand-buffed teal vase, or the local weaver for a shimmering, red-carpet-ready cactus-fibre evening wrap. Purchases from travellers have helped keep these vital traditions alive, and continue to push Marrakshi *maâlems* to innovate in an extremely competitive artisans' market.

In Marrakesh, traditional craftsmanship is anything but stodgy. Skilled Marrakshi artisans are often hired by European, Japanese and American designers to execute their ideas, and in turn Marrakshi artisans gain exposure to cutting-edge design from around the world. The result is a polyglot Marrakesh modernism with deep, saturated Moroccan hues, mod organic shapes, and spare geometric and Berber motifs. This inspiration has recently emerged in painting and sculpture, which used to be lesser Moroccan art forms but are now major attractions at Nouvelle Ville galleries, along with ultramodern calligraphy. Go on and add your ideas to the artistic mix: courses in crafts and culinary arts are offered at a number of riads.

## BEST PLACES TO SEE MAÂLEMS AT WORK
> The souq circuit (p81)
> Ensemble Artisanal (p40)
> Fondouqs (p98)
> Masroure Abdillah (p102)
> Abdelatif Instruments (p83)

## BEST CRAFTS YOU WON'T FIND AT HOME
> Carpet weaving: Ensemble Artisanal (p40)
> *Passimenterie* (hand-knotted trims and tassels): Couleurs Orientales Marrakesh (p112)
> Stucco (plasterwork): Sidi Ahmad Gabaz Stucco (p86)
> *Tadelakt*: Creation Chez Lamine (p100)
> Tyre crafts: Creations Pneumatiques (p112)

## BEST 'NOT SO TRADITIONAL' TRADITIONAL ARTS
> Kifkif (p100)
> Matisse Art Gallery (p41)
> Ministero del Gusto (p102)
> Galerie Noir Sur Blanc (p40)
> Sidi Ghanem (p46)

## BEST PLACES TO LEARN FROM LOCAL MASTERS
> Dar Attajmil (p120)
> Jnane Tamsna (p66)
> La Maison Arabe (p124)
> Riad Bledna (p66)
> Riad Sahara Nour (p127)

**Top left** Touching up the *zellij* in the Bahia Palace (p108)

# BERBER CULTURE

Before there were kings, spice traders, or even carpet sellers here, central Morocco was home to the Amazigh, or 'free people' of Saharan, Mediterranean and sub-Saharan African origin. The Romans tried to conquer the Amazigh for 250 years. When they couldn't defeat their foes they badmouthed them, dubbing them 'Berbers' or Barbarians.

The Berber Pride movement has recently reclaimed 'Berber' as a unifying term, and Marrakesh proudly claims Berber roots. Tashelhit is the most common Berber language, and it's widely spoken in Marrakesh: road-test Tashelhit greetings (see p73) and earn a warm welcome for your pronunciation troubles. In the Rahba Qedima you'll see Berber remedies for everything from excess nerdiness (walnut root) to marital issues (galanga). The Berber carpets festooning the souqs were traditionally woven by women for wedding trousseaus, so they often feature symbols warding off bad luck (ie unworthy grooms) and promoting domestic bliss.

One thing you can't buy at any price is *baraka*, loosely described as a state of grace. As one Berber herbalist explains, '*Baraka* doesn't grow on trees – it comes from what you do' (see below for *baraka*-enhancing hints). Aficionados claim that when you've got *baraka*, you're more in sync with your surroundings, people pick up your good vibes and life seems sweeter. '*Barakallahlekoum*' ('*baraka* be with you').

## BEST PLACES TO EXPERIENCE BERBER CULTURE

> Imlil and other High Atlas villages (p146)
> Imilchil Marriage Festival (p25) and other *moussems* (celebrations)
> Djemaa el-Fna (p10)
> Maison Tiskiwin (p110)
> Dar Taliba (p157)

## BEST WAYS TO GET BARAKA

> Donations to Dar Taliba or other Berber village projects (p157)
> Exchanging Berber pleasantries (see p73)
> Buying from local cooperatives (p113)
> Conserving water to help High Atlas subsistence farmers (p156)
> Tipping Gnaoua musicians and storytellers in the Djemaa (p10)

# CLUBS & BARS

By day it's all serene palaces and hardworking souqs, but at night Marrakesh will not rest until a good time is had by all – hence the Ibiza-esque hours of most entertainment venues here and the essential midafternoon nap. Around 11pm, Marrakshis turn Nouvelle Ville restaurants into impromptu discos, bars into sing-along stages and outdoor cafés into hook-up hot spots. Many bars are still male dominated, but several actively encourage women to attend with free drinks – take advantage now, before they do the maths. From here it's on to Pacha Marrakesh (p59) or Le Théâtro (p59) until dawn, then a hammam and nap poolside in the Palmeraie to dry out until happy hour.

The Marrakesh nightlife scene has a speakeasy feel – and technically, there are still Moroccan laws on the books against extramarital sex, homosexuality and selling alcohol within view of a mosque (ie everywhere, especially in the Medina). But once night falls and the music starts, cocktails flow on discreet Medina terraces and in thumping Guéliz bars, and glances are traded across crowded Hivernage dance floors. Mind you, certain come-hither looks in almost any Marrakesh watering hole – especially the high-end ones – are strictly professional. At the risk of stating the obvious, steer clear of paid company, so the only thing you'll have to regret tomorrow is that fourth Moroccan mint mojito.

## BEST WATERING HOLES
> Jad Mahal (p57)
> Bô Zin (p56)
> Kosybar (p115)
> Le Foundouk (p87)
> Abyssin (p64; pictured above)

## BEST DANCE-FLOOR ACTION
> Pacha Marrakesh (p59)
> Le Comptoir (p55)
> Diamant Noir (p57)
> Actor's (p56)
> Le Théâtro (p59)

# FAITH & TRADITION

Soaring minarets, intricate calligraphy, mesmerising calls to prayer: much of what thrills visitors to Marrakesh is inspired by faith. As part of their religious practice, many Muslim Marrakshis make time for quiet reflection and prayer, raucous Ramadan celebrations (you're invited; see below) and everyday kindness – *zakat* (charity) is one of the five pillars of Islam. Marrakesh has seven *marabouts* (patron saints), but *marabouts' zaouias* (shrines) are closed to non-Muslims, as are Marrakesh mosques. But one of the most historic religious sites is open to visitors: the spectacular Ali ben Youssef Medersa (p80), a former college of Islamic learning and law.

Marrakesh's crossroads culture draws from interfaith influences. Follow your senses through the streets of Marrakesh and you'll glimpse ancient animist beliefs in Berber homeopathic cures, taste salty, pickled Jewish culinary influences in local cuisine, and hear Gnaoua riffs and rhythms that predate the arrival of Islam in Africa. Wander through Marrakesh's 700-year-old Mellah, or Jewish quarter, and you'll come across Star of David doorknockers, a still-functioning ancient synagogue, and the Miaâra (Jewish cemetery; p111). Christian and Jewish communities have been established in Morocco for some 1700 years, and they're still active in the Nouvelle Ville at a synagogue, Catholic church and Protestant hall. Multiple religious traditions have inspired an outpouring of creativity in Marrakesh, and the city's rich traditions of poetry, folk dance, storytelling and street theatre offer roles for one and all.

## BEST WAYS TO CELEBRATE RAMADAN

> Party in the streets on Aïd el-Fitr (p164)
> Wake up for the predawn adhan from Koutoubia Minaret (p16)
> Practise *zakat*: donate to a worthy local cause (p157)
> Avoid eating, drinking and smoking in front of hungry, thirsty, jonesing hosts by day (p30)
> Binge on sweets and *harira* (lentil soup) after sunset in the souqs (p12)

## BEST LOCAL TRADITIONS IN ACTION

> *Halqa* (street theatre): Djemaa el-Fna (p10)
> Literature/storytelling: Café du Livre (p54)
> Fusion Moroccan cuisine: Dar Moha (p93)
> Berber remedies: Dar Taliba (p157)
> Folk music: Marrakesh Festival of Popular Arts (p25)

# GARDENS

When Yusuf bin Tachfin and his fierce Almoravid warriors swept into a campsite now known as Marrakesh, the first thing they did was start to garden. The Almoravids set up the ingenious *khattara* irrigation system that watered royal gardens and still supports the Palmeraie. Today the gardens nurtured by those combative nature-lovers have become a distinguishing feature of the city, from the grand Menara Gardens (p41) to intimate riad courtyards. There's a garden to suit every style: foodies can dine in Nouvelle Ville garden restaurants (p47), sports fans can play tennis and football in Jardin Harti (p58) and stress cases can unwind in the Palmeraie oasis (p62).

With so many gardens, pools and golf courses taxing the millennium-old *khattara* system and tapping water reserves (see p156), Marrakshi gardeners are getting resourceful with grey-water reuse systems and water-conserving plants. One model garden is at Dar Taliba (p157), the nonprofit Berber girls' school in the High Atlas where students learn to identify and cultivate indigenous herbs. Girls who once had no chance of attending school have gone on to study ethno-botany, and compiled a definitive catalogue of Berber medicinal herbs. For a donation, visitors can tour the garden, enjoy some healing tea and find botanical bliss.

## BEST MARRAKESH GARDEN ACTIVITIES

> Check email at Cyberpark (p37)
> Enjoy high tea or highballs at sunset in the garden at Bar du Soleil in the Mamounia Hotel (p54)
> Join a *koura* (football) match at Jardin Harti (p58)
> Dine on garden-fresh organic cuisine at Jnane Tamsna (p133)
> Find fresh gardening ideas at Jardin'Art Garden Festival (p24)

## BEST GARDENS FOR...

> Inspiration: Dar Taliba (p157)
> Romance: Menara Gardens (p41)
> Art: Jardin Majorelle (p41)
> Royal sightings: Agdal Gardens (p108)
> Kids: Jardin Harti (p58)

# KIDS

The mutual admiration between kids and Marrakesh is obvious. Kids will gaze in wonderment at fairy-tale souq scenes their parents pretend to take in their stride: potion sellers trading concoctions straight out of *Harry Potter,* old tins being hammered into Aladdin-esque lamps, cupboard-sized shops packed with spangled slippers worthy of Cinderella. Since most Marrakshis dote on kids, yours may emerge from the souqs thoroughly spoiled by all the attention, their pockets bulging with treats and faces smeared with sweets.

There's plenty to stimulate young minds and reward good behaviour after a day of sightseeing. Active imaginations go wild in splendid palaces and kids get a second wind with treats from Ice Legend (p72) or Oliveri (p52). Kids used to leashed pets and packaged meats will surely be surprised to see animals wandering about, pulling carts or being sold in markets – and this could be the start of a most educational conversation. When grownup company becomes tiresome, gardens are usually good for impromptu play dates. For family fun, try camel safaris, pony rides and bowling in the Palmeraie (p64).

Marrakesh's facilities aren't always ideal for kids – riads with unattended plunge pools, steep steps and low electrical outlets aren't child-proof – and bear in mind that some of your fellow guests in intimate riad quarters may not take kindly to boisterous toddlers. To find the most kid-friendly venues, look for the 👶 symbol throughout this guide. See individual reviews for babysitting services, and ask about English-speaking services when booking.

## BEST TREATS
> Ice Legend (p72)
> Alrazal (p42)
> Amandine (p48)
> Gnaoua Music Shop (p112)
> Tesoruccio (p47)

## BEST HANGOUTS
> Kawkab Jeux (p58)
> Tesoruccio Playground (p60)
> Cyberpark (p37)
> Jardin Harti (p58)

# PAMPERING

Radiant skin and relaxed attitudes are far more common than you'd expect this close to the Sahara in the midst of souq traffic – and for that, you can thank the *tebbaya*. A *tebbaya* is the hero of the hammam (traditional Moroccan bathhouse) who performs the essential *gommage,* the exfoliating treatment done with gummy *savon noir* (literally 'black soap'; natural palm soap) and a *kessa* (rough-textured glove).

A hammam might sound decadent, but it's one of the best deals in Marrakesh. Entry and *gommage* cost just Dh30 to Dh50 at a community hammam (expect to pay Dh150-plus at a riad hammam). And you'll leave with a clean conscience, too: once the day's steam gets going, a gorgeous *gommage* uses fewer resources than most showers. At any community hammam, you'll need your own plastic mat, flip-flops, towel and a change of undies – you'll be expected to wear yours so they'll get wet.

You might also opt for *rhassoul*, a mud scalp rub, or a massage with healing oils of argan (for stressed-out skin) or arnica (for sore muscles). Fancy hammams in the Palmeraie and Nouvelle Ville offer speciality treatments including Jacuzzis, facials with local herbs, and four-handed massages with two masseurs plying sore muscles. Women traditionally get henna tattoos to mark celebrations in Marrakesh, and your vacation is surely an occasion to celebrate. But be sure to avoid 'black henna', a mix of synthetic dyes that can cause your skin to blister – go with all-natural (aka 'red' or 'green') henna instead. See p18 for more.

## BEST AUTHENTIC HAMMAMS

> Hammam Bab Doukkala (p95)
> Hammam Dar el-Bacha (p95)
> Bain d'Or (p89)
> Les Deux Tours Hammam (p66)
> Les Palais Rhoul Hammam (p67)

## BEST MOROCCAN SPA TREATMENTS

> *Gommage*: Hammam Dar el-Bacha (p95)
> Four-handed massage: Sultana Spa (p116)
> Threading: Maison Arabe (p95)
> Mineral salt scrubs: Les Secrets de Marrakesh (p58)
> Henna: Rahba Qedima (p83)

V

# PERFORMING ARTS

All the world may be a stage, but Marrakesh has been stealing the show for 1000 years. *Halqa* (street theatre) performers make you stop and stare at triple flips, gyrating cobras and belly dancers with double-jointed hips. When an act is riveting, an encore is assured by providing generous tips.

Movies are not your average multiplex fare here. You'll see Marrakshis lining up for independent films at Institut Français (p57) and all-male crowds singing along to Bollywood musicals at Cinéma Eden (p77). The crowd goes wild at the Marrakesh International Film Festival (p26) – especially at open-air screenings in the Djemaa el-Fna.

Many restaurants feature live music and belly dancing nightly. Technically, belly dancing is an Ottoman tradition, but in Djemaa el-Fna they aren't hung up on such technicalities; enjoyment and expression are it.

The city's cultural institutions also put on quite a show. Big-name acts perform at Théâtre Royal (p60), Institut Français (p57) and Dar Chérifa (p98). Moroccan stars take to the streets at the Marrakesh Festival of Popular Arts (p25) and you can also discover local acts on CDs at Kifkif (p100) and Le Comptoir (p55).

## BEST LIVE PERFORMANCES
> Djemaa el-Fna (p10)
> Marrakesh Festival of Popular Arts (p25)
> Théâtre Royal (p60)
> Institut Français (p57)
> Openings at Dar Chérifa (p98)

## BEST FOR MUSIC
> Djemaa el-Fna (p10)
> Essaouira Gnaoua Music Festival (p24)
> Théâtre Royal (p60)
> Rencontres Musicales de Marrakech (p24)
> Essaouira Alizés (Trade Winds) Classical Music Festival (p24)

## BEST VENUES FOR DANCE
> Djemaa el-Fna (p10)
> Riad Sahara Nour (p127)
> Institut Français (p57)
> Théâtre Royal (p60)
> Marrakesh Festival of Popular Arts (p25)

## BEST MOVIE MAGIC
> Marrakesh International Film Festival (p26)
> Cinéma Colisée (p56)
> The perfume 'Festival' at Les Parfums du Soleil (p45)
> Film Fest after parties at Actor's (p56)
> Institut Français (p57)

# SHOPPING

Who knew shopping could be so enlightening? You can glimpse a *maâlem's* mosaic techniques, learn Berber sunburn remedies from apothecaries and get the ceremonial mint-tea treatment in carpet shops. You can probably get that pillowcase made to match your sofa or a suit tailored to fit, and artisans will proudly show you how it's done. Factor friendly banter into your shopping time for a warm reception and probably a better price – everything is negotiable in the souqs except obligatory pleasantries. Whether you buy or not, the shopkeeper will remember you tomorrow, and greet you with '*Labes?*' ('Happy?') At these prices, who wouldn't be?

The two barriers to a Marrakshi overhaul of your home décor and wardrobe are cash and shipping. Credit cards and travellers cheques are usually not accepted in the souqs. Some Medina merchants might offer you 'Berber credit', where you pay most of the purchase price and take your purchase, returning with the balance later. Shoppers pressed for time will prefer fixed (though usually higher) prices and credit-card machines in the Nouvelle Ville. It can cost as much as you paid for your carpet to ship it home, so travel with empty suitcases.

Most shops in the souqs open by 10am and stay open until 7pm, only closing on Friday afternoon. Nouvelle Ville stores are open Monday to Saturday by 10am, close from 1.30pm to 3.30pm, then open again until 7pm.

## BEST BARGAIN GIFTS

> Essential oil soaps from L'Art du Bain Savonnerie Artisanale (p102)
> Hand beaten felt flowers from Masroure Abdillah (p102)
> Mini tagines from Mademoiselle Ibtissam's Original Design (p113)
> Tigmi Cooperative coasters from Jamade (p112)
> Jewellery boxes of responsibly sourced thuya wood from Cooperative Artisanale Femmes de Marrakech (p84)

## BEST SOUVENIRS THAT AREN'T CARPETS

> Michelin tyre photo-frame from Creations Pneumatiques (p112), featuring your best souq shot
> 18-spice blend from Mouhassin Epices (p113)
> Argan massage oil from Assouss Cooperative d'Argane (p99)
> Recycled metal castanets from Gnaoua Music Shop (p112)
> Moroccan sardine-tin mirror from Kifkif (p100)

V

# SPORT & ADVENTURE

As if laps of the souqs weren't enough of a workout, Marrakesh packs in adventures for the hyperactive. You can find tennis, fellow joggers and stadium football in Jardin Harti (p58), and pickup football games on almost any spare patch of *piste* (hard-packed earth). The Palmeraie offers more sporting options: horseback riding, camel rides, and less frenetic roads for bicyclists and serious marathoners than in town. Swimming, gyms and exercise classes are mostly limited to Nouvelle Ville hotels or Palmeraie guesthouses. Gym junkies can try Canal Forme (p56), a gym/spa open to nonmembers. But in the dry midday heat, most locals leave physical feats of daring to the acrobats in the Djemaa el-Fna.

Great outdoor adventures await just outside Marrakesh in the mountain villages around picturesque Imlil, hidden oases of the High Atlas, and the pre-Saharan desert. While you can't get to Saharan dunes in a weekend from Marrakesh without harrowingly reckless driving over mountain passes, you can get a breathtaking desert experience in an afternoon in the Agafay Desert, 40km from Marrakesh. In this desert, La Pause (p133) offers overnight stays, organic meals and eco-friendly all-terrain golf, and **Inside Morocco Travel** (www.insidemoroccotravel.com) hosts picnics in a Berber ghost town. Ask eco-travel guide Mohamed Nour about combining this picnic with an overnight stay in Imlil and his 'Secret Valleys Tour', visiting Berber villages that cling to cliffs in High Atlas oases.

## BEST LOCAL SPORTS

> All-terrain golf and disc golf in the desert at La Pause (www.lapause-marrakech.com)
> *Koura* in Jardin Harti (p58)
> Running the Marathon of Marrakesh (p24)
> Horseback, camel and bike riding in the Palmeraie (p64)
> Bargaining in the souqs (p12)

## BEST QUICK ADVENTURES

> High Atlas treks near Imlil (www.insidemoroccotravel.com)
> Ghost town picnics in the Comune de Agafay Desert (www.insidemoroccotravel.com)
> Essaouira beach break by bus (p160)
> Diversity Excursions to the Saharan oasis of Skoura (www.diversity-excursions.co.uk)
> Imilchil Marriage Festival (p25)

The souqs: always entertaining

# BACKGROUND

## HISTORY

Youssef ben Tachfine, the brilliant Almoravid strategist who conquered Spain, saw potential in this trading post strategically located between the desert, mountains and the sea and built ramparts around it in 1062. His son Ali ben Youssef's dedication to prayer, fasting and construction projects did wonders for the city's architecture and irrigation systems – but not so much for the Almoravids' military standing against the Almohads, a rival Berber tribe. The Almohads' founder was tossed out of Mecca for berating pilgrims who weren't praying hard enough. These pious pillagers swept into town in 1147, razing the first Koutoubia Mosque, which was mis-aligned with Mecca, but mysteriously leaving the Koubba Ba'adiyn intact.

Under Almohad Yacoub el-Mansour (the Victorious), Marrakesh became an imperial capital with a fortified Kasbah, new mosques (the rebuilt Koutoubia Mosque and the Kasbah Mosque), glorious gardens (including the Menara and Agdal Gardens), *qissarias* (covered markets) and a triumphal gate (Bab Agnaou) – only to lose it all to the Merenids, who preferred Meknès and Fez. After two centuries as a capital, Marrakesh was reduced to its humble origins as a trading outpost. By the time the Saadians took control in the early 16th century, the city was decimated by famine.

### SWEET & SOUR

Sugar made life sweet again when the Saadians made Marrakesh the focal point of their lucrative sugar trade route. Sultan Moulay Abdallah created a Jewish quarter (the Mellah) outside the Kasbah in 1558 and a trading centre for Christians – generous gifts that these communities repaid many times over in taxes. With the proceeds, the Sultan rebuilt the Almoravid Ali ben Youssef Mosque and Medersa. His successor, Ahmed el-Mansour Eddahbi (the Victorious and Golden), had more worldly ambitions, paving the Badi Palace with gold and precious stones, and taking opulence to the grave with the sumptuous Saadian Tombs.

But as any storyteller in the Djemaa el-Fna might've predicted, the good life wouldn't last for Marrakesh. The city lapsed into lawlessness until the Arab Alawites brought long-term stability (the current king is descended from this dynasty). But Marrakshis might have preferred anarchy to early Alawite leader Moulay Ismail, whose idea of fun was performing amateur dentistry on anyone who irked him. Lucky for Marrakshis fond of their teeth, Moulay Ismail preferred docile Meknès to unruly Marrakesh, and moved his headquarters there – though not before looting the Badi Palace.

## PALACES & PIE

Marrakesh entered its Wild West period, when big guns vied for control over local trades in goods and slaves. Those who prevailed built extravagant riads, but the Medina walls were left to crumble, once-grand gardens filled with garbage and much of the population lived hand to mouth in crowded *fondouqs* (rooming houses). In the 19th century Sultan Moulay Hassan built the extravagant Bahia Palace, bankrolled by increasingly disgruntled Marrakshi taxpayers.

Meanwhile, European colonial powers began breaking off pieces of North Africa like hunks of tasty *bastilla* (pigeon pie). Sultan Moulay Abdelaziz tried to ally with the British, but Britain abandoned Abdelaziz to contend with the French, the Spanish and his own people, who'd had enough of paying taxes to bankroll his expensive European tastes.

A local Berber warlord named Thami el-Glaoui proved much more adept at bartering with the French and repressing his own people. In 1912 the French résident-général anointed Thami el-Glaoui pasha of Marrakesh with impunity to do as he wished, which included extorting protection money, executing rivals, kidnapping women and children who struck his fancy, and playing golf with Ike Eisenhower and Winston Churchill. Legend has it that before the pasha left Marrakesh to attend Queen Elizabeth II's coronation, a fresh display of human heads decorated his palace to dissuade nationalists agitating for independence. The heads didn't work, nor did exiling nationalist sympathiser King Mohammed V. The pasha came to a bitter end in 1956, wracked with cancer and begging the King's forgiveness.

## IMPERIAL AGAIN

The new constitutional monarchy was established by Mohammed V and taken over in 1961 by his controversial son Hassan II. In 1975 Hassan II ordered the Green March, a protest march of 350,000 Moroccan citizens from Marrakesh into Western Sahara to establish Morocco's claim on the former Spanish colony (and its phosphate and oil resources), which sparked an ongoing conflict. With a growing gap between rich and poor, and a mounting tax bill to cover military debt, Hassan II suppressed trade unionists, women's rights activists, Islamists, journalists, Berbers and the working poor – a cross-section of Moroccan society – which led to mass protests in 1981. Hundreds were killed, 1000 wounded, and an estimated 5000 protesters arrested in a nationwide *laraf* (roundup).

At the urging of Morocco's human rights advocates, the extreme measures of Hassan II's black years have been curbed by Mohammed VI. Today Morocco has one of the best reputations for human rights in the Middle East and Africa, with specific prohibitions against torture and a Justice and Reconciliation Commission. Municipal and parliamentary elections have been introduced, as well as 2004 amendments to the Islamic-based 'Mudawwana' civil laws concerning marriage, divorce and custodial rights. But crackdowns on the press were revived before the 2007 parliamentary elections and only about a third of the electorate voted – a percentage many pundits construe as a no-confidence vote. But while Rabat takes two steps forward, one step back, Marrakesh hurtles forward as the capital of Morocco's tourism industry, with a cosmopolitan outlook that's true to its history and promising for its future.

# LIFE AS A MARRAKSHI

For a millennia-old civilization, Marrakesh sure looks young for its age. There's a reason for this, beyond all those rejuvenating hammams: over half Morocco's population is under 20 years old. Primary education to

## MARRAKSHI SOCIAL GRACES

> Do accept mint tea whenever it's offered, even if you just take a sip.
> Do avoid clingy or revealing clothes, whether you're a man or a woman. Many Marrakshis wear skimpy clothes, especially to clubs. But if you do, you'll be avoided by elderly Marrakshis, who were raised when attire indicated education, morality and a certain profession – and you'll be missing out on excellent company.
> Do greet Marrakshis you've met warmly: shake hands, then touch your heart with your right hand. Women may kiss one another on the cheek three times, and men clasp one another's hands for a long, long time. Men and women might exchange a handshake and air-kiss if they're good friends.
> Don't drink alcohol in public areas; if there's a mosque nearby (and there usually is), it's considered insensitive.
> Don't smooch in public. Even hand-holding between men and women makes many locals uncomfortable – though it's common between men who are friends, and among women as well.
> Don't take pictures without asking permission first. Many Muslims believe that humans are created in God's image, and attempting to capture God's reflection is hubris. Other objections are strictly practical, including Marrakshi artisans concerned others may copy their designs.

the age of 14 is now required and model initiatives around Marrakesh are working hard to reduce female illiteracy rates as high as 60% – Moroccan girls account for almost 66% of the half a million Moroccan children under the age of 15 who work instead of getting an education. To help keep kids in school, make purchases only from adults; don't give kids handouts – it teaches them to beg and shames their parents, so consider charities listed in the boxed text (p157) instead; and, at the risk of sounding like your own grandma, urge kids to study hard.

While Moroccan society revolves around the family, young Moroccans are increasingly leaving home and delaying marriage to pursue careers in Marrakesh. Not that it's always easy to find jobs: unemployment for Moroccans aged 25 to 44 years approaches 20%. Moroccans living in France, Germany, Spain and the USA – whose remittances to family back home represent as much as 20% of GDP – are increasingly sponsoring family members to pursue studies and careers abroad. But for go-getters in the booming hospitality sector, Marrakesh offers exceptional opportunity.

## AIMING TO PLEASE

Seven days a week, no matter how early you rise in the morning, there's already someone in the souqs (covered market streets) to greet you in several languages: 'Hello, come in, you're welcome in Marrakesh'. This isn't just lip service – historically Marrakesh is a crossroads culture, where the dominant Berber population mingled with Arabs and Gnaoua (freed slaves from sub-Saharan Africa). The city's now-small Christian and Jewish populations are almost as old as the city itself, and Europeans have been a constant presence for more than a century. But though cosmopolitan locals won't be surprised to see you, they'll certainly be pleased: your visit duly honours their culture and their city, and your contributions go a long way in an economy where the minimum hourly wage is Dh3.2.

While you're in town, you'll encounter some of the many European, American and even a few Kiwi expatriates running riads – and incurring a certain amount of resentment for buying up prime Medina real estate, inflating local prices and not paying their fair share of taxes. In turn, some expats accuse locals of narrow-mindedness, so be prepared to take generalizations you hear on either side with a hefty grain of Essaouira sea salt. But cultural differences are not insurmountable in Marrakesh – witness the many intercultural couples you'll meet running riads, restaurants and other businesses.

## MAKE MERRY & BE BAHJA

It's not all work and no play for Marrakshis, known across Morocco as the *bahja* (joyous ones). Marrakshis are generous with their time and extend courtesies that might seem to you like impositions, from walking you to your next destination so you don't get lost to inviting you home for tea or lunch. Most nights out are group outings with family or friends, but you'll witness dates in progress in gardens and quiet upper terraces of cafés – and plenty of smoochy faces made via webcam in internet cafés. Among the regular Marrakesh cybercafé crowds of instant messagers, bloggers and internet daters are plenty of Moroccan women, who now account for 30% of all Arab women on the internet. Marrakesh's literati are hardly stuffy, and a good time is had by all at literary café and Nouvelle Ville gallery openings. But when Marrakshis take over the streets for festivals, open-air movie screenings and nightly performances in the Djemaa el-Fna, everyone becomes *bahja* (joyous).

# ARTS & ARCHITECTURE

Arts aren't a specialised, lofty pursuit here; they're the bright thread that runs through the fabric of Marrakshi life. To track the latest Moroccan cultural developments, check out the Morocco page of the award-

---

### WOMEN IN MARRAKESH

Marrakesh is becoming a destination of choice among women travellers, and it's a comparatively safer place to visit solo than London or New York. What with the plain-clothes police, staff at your riad or hotel, and locals you befriend, someone is always keeping an eye out for you. Marrakshi men are often more respectful than the blokes back home; it may be off-putting to be called 'gazelle', but it's fairly innocuous. Unwanted interactions are easy to end: just walk away. Souq shopkeepers may occasionally tap your shoulder, but otherwise you won't be touched by anyone you don't know. If you ever do feel threatened or harassed, just shout '*Aib!*' (shame). This will get the attention of anyone within earshot, and the provocateur will very likely run away.

Follow the etiquette guidelines (see the boxed text, p150) and you'll soon be at ease among Marrakshi women and men alike. This is a privilege male travellers do not often enjoy, since male-female interactions are still stilted by social convention. Women visitors may meet Marrakshiyyas (Marrakesh women) eager to chat, compare life experiences and exchange ideas about world events. Marrakshiyyas are having their say and taking charge as never before, and you can show your support by visiting Marrakshiyya-run businesses such as Al Fassia (p47) and women's cooperatives (see the boxed text, p113).

## LANDMARK SPOTTING

Head to a Medina riad or restaurant rooftop and see if you can spot these local architectural landmarks:

**Fondouqs** Medieval courtyard compounds that house artisans' workshops downstairs, and travellers, traders and workers upstairs.

**Riads** Mud-brick courtyard mansions, traditionally centred around a garden with a fountain.

**Zaouias** *Marabout* (saint) shrines closed to non-Muslims; you'll notice their green-tiled roofs pointing heavenward in the northern Medina.

**Hammams** Domed public bathhouses let off steam through star-shaped vents, traditionally lined with *tadelakt* (polished plaster).

**Fountains** Local water sources supplied by ingenious underground irrigation systems sustained Marrakesh through years-long medieval sieges.

winning European-based www.babelmed.net, which features articles on new books, films, travelling art shows, and UN reports in French and English.

## ARCHITECTURE

Marrakshi mud-brick architecture may be low to the ground, but it's a monumental achievement. Metre-thick walls absorb heat to keep buildings cool in summer and warm in winter – and building materials don't get much more green than local mud mixed with straw for strength. Buildings more than one storey tall are reinforced with cedar posts and capped with rooftop terraces, where neighbours catch breezes and local gossip in the evenings.

## LITERATURE

Watch the storytellers, singers and scribes in the Djemaa el-Fna, and you'll understand how Morocco's literary tradition has remained so vital and irrepressible. William S Burroughs, Paul Bowles and other Beat Generation authors were inspired by the city's storytelling traditions – but Marrakesh also looms large in the Moroccan literary imagination, notably in Marrakshi Mahi Binebine's harrowing 2003 novel *Welcome to Paradise* and Moroccan author Tahar ben Jelloun's Prix Goncourt–winning novel *The Sand Child*. Sociologist Fatima Mernissi, Moroccan feminist and author of the memoir *Dreams of Trespass: Tales of a Harem Girlhood*, memorably describes Marrakesh as 'the city where black and white legends crossed, languages mingled and religions clashed with the immutable silence of the dancing sands'. So may it be again: despite recent press censorship, poetry readings, literary cafés, book clubs and small publishers are springing up in Marrakesh.

## MUSIC

Loud, heartfelt and irresistibly funky Gnaoua music vies for listeners' attention with subtle, Berber-inflected Andalucian classical music, but both reward close listening. Classical musicians strum chords from lutes and ouds that resonate as though they're being played on your heartstrings instead. At times the music speeds up like a racing heartbeat, only to subside to a single note that follows you all the way home. Gnaoua musicians thrum out catchy, bluesy tunes on handmade instruments, including metal castanets, *ribabs* (three-stringed banjos) and plenty of *deffs* (hand-held drums), working themselves and their audience into a joyous trance. The tradition was started in Marrakesh and Essaouira as a ritual of deliverance from slavery that sets spirits free. Lately the big names on the Marrakesh music scene are women's, namely the all-women group B'net Marrakech, and the bold Najat Aatabou, who's the Berber Bob Dylan with her poetic protest songs.

## CRAFTS

Marrakshi applied arts and architecture have left viewers agog for centuries, but the recent rage for riad décor has created a visual bonanza in the following art forms.

Carpets and textiles – anything that isn't nailed down in Morocco is likely to be woven, sewn or embroidered, and even then it might be upholstered. Moroccan women are the under-recognised *maâlems* (expert craftspeople) of Moroccan textiles: check out Berber carpets and evening wraps made of *sabra* (cactus silk).

Ceramics – Marrakesh doesn't have much of a ceramics tradition, but has proved a quick study with monochrome Berber-style ceramics, which emphasize striking forms over elaborate decoration.

Woodwork – riad doors and palace ceilings are traditionally made of cedar, and orangewood makes fragrant *harira* (lentil soup) ladles. Knotty, caramel-coloured thuya (conifer indigenous to Morocco) wood is at risk of being admired to extinction, so consider buying thuya crafts from artisans' collectives likely to practise responsible collection and reforesting, such as Cooperative Artisanale Femmes de Marrakech (p84).

**THE FINE PRINT**

Calligraphy is one of Marrakesh's most cherished art forms and if you look closely, you'll notice the same text by different calligraphers has an incredibly different effect. One might take up a whole page with a single word, while another might fold it origami-style into a flower. The slanting cursive script most commonly used for the Quran is Naskh; cursive letters ingeniously interlaced to form a shape or dense design are hallmarks of the Thuluth style; and high-impact graphic lettering is the Kufic style from Iraq that comes knotted, foliate (vine-like) or square. Check out Galerie Noir Sur Blanc (p40) for abstract modern styles and invent your own style at calligraphy workshops at Riad Bledna (p66).

Metalwork – pierced brass lamps, iron lanterns and votive candle-holders of recycled sardine tins create instant atmosphere. Any proper Moroccan tea ceremony requires just the right props: gleaming brass teapots and tea trays, engraved and highly polished to reflect well on hosts.

*Zellij* – puzzle-work mosaic takes decades to perfect, but look out Fez: thanks to the riad décor craze, Marrakshi *maâlems* have more opportunity to hone their craft than Fassi masters.

## CONTEMPORARY ART

Nonfunctional sculpture and figurative painting used to be a lesser artistic tradition in Marrakesh, catering to tourist demands for kitschy blue-veiled Tuareg figurines and Delacroix-derivative paintings of musket-toting horsemen. But now such works are widely dismissed as trying too hard to fit the 'exotic Moroccan' mould, and serious Marrakshi galleries are taking more risks with cutting-edge calligraphy (see boxed text, above), painting and installations. It doesn't hurt that Mohammed VI takes a personal interest in contemporary Moroccan art either.

# GOVERNMENT & POLITICS

Marrakshis are known for being outspoken and you'll hear lively political debates in the souqs. The famed 'Berber bluntness' can be refreshing or challenging, depending on which side of the argument you're on, but Marrakshis are consistently generous about differentiating between people and politics. One of the first questions you'll be asked is 'Where are you from?' Whether your answer is Britain, the USA, Afghanistan or Zanzibar, the response is always the same: 'You are welcome in Marrakesh'.

The talk in Marrakesh is well ahead of the political curve in Rabat. Marrakesh's municipal council remains subject to Rabat's control, and draconian new Moroccan antiterrorism laws have been criticised by Amnesty International. Marrakshis are known for irreverent humour, but the King is not amused: in 2007, Mohammed VI banned the popular Moroccan publication *Nichane* for a cover article called 'Jokes: How Moroccans Laugh at Religion, Sex and Politics', and an issue of the Moroccan weekly *TelQuel* was pulped for 'failing to respect' the King. But crackdowns don't stop Marrakshis from speaking their minds behind closed doors or jokesters in the souqs from daring wisecracks.

# ENVIRONMENT

Many of Morocco's 40,000 wildlife species thrive in the oasis ecosystem of Marrakesh – but there is trouble in paradise. Two of the three major reservoirs in southern Morocco have run dry and Morocco now has a third of the water resources of Iraq. Environmentalist Mohammed el Faïz points out the irony that the ultimate garden city – 'the rose amid the palms' – has become both victim and perpetrator of what he calls 'patrimonial vandalism', with lush new real-estate developments demanding ever more water from High Atlas subsistence farmers. According to the Centre for Environmental Systems Research, Morocco ranks in the top 25 nations under the most severe water stress, above the Sudan and Mexico.

## GO EASY ON THE ENVIRONMENT

Here's how you can make your holiday low-stress for both you and Marrakesh's delicate desert environment:

**Reduce your 'wet footprint'** Ask hotel/riad staff to change your linens weekly instead of daily, stay at places with small plunge pools instead of Olympic ones, and enjoy a steamy public hammam instead of a long shower.

**Improve your golf game with all-terrain golfing** La Pause (p133) offers a rare opportunity to golf as nature intended, on a spectacular turfless course in the Agafay Desert. Marrakesh can't spare the water for the three turf golf courses it already has, let alone three more planned in Oukaïmeden – consider donating 'green fees' instead to local Berber village projects (see boxed text, opposite).

**Venture off the grid** Sleep under the stars on gridskipping trips with **Authentic Discoveries** (www.authenticdiscoveries.com), **Mountain Voyages** (www.mountain-voyage.com) or **Inside Morocco Travel** (www.insidemoroccotravel.com).

## GIVE IT UP FOR MARRAKESH: FOUR WORTHY CAUSES

**Global Diversity Foundation** (www.globaldiversity.org.uk) A UK-based organisation that promotes biodiversity and cultural diversity in the Marrakesh area.

**AlterEgo** (www.alterego-maroc.com; 22 Rue de Yougoslavie) This Marrakesh NGO connects local NGO initiatives with people who want to help (hey, that's you).

**Reporters without Borders** (www.rsf.org) Supports Moroccan journalists who face fines, harassment, even prison time for publishing articles that diverge from official party lines.

**Dar Taliba** (El Hanchane, near Imlil) The ground-breaking girls' school gives rural girls access to middle-school education and keeps essential Berber botanical knowledge alive; see it featured on the BBC gardening show **Ground Forces** (www.bbc.co.uk/gardening/tv_and _radio/gforce_marrakech.shtml).

# FURTHER READING

*Hope and Other Dangerous Pursuits* is Laila Lalami's celebrated novel about the dreams and fateful decisions of Moroccan immigrants.

Esther Freud's *Hideous Kinky* is a childhood memoir of a magical, haunting two-year pit stop in 1960s Marrakesh along the Hippie Trail.

Catch Moroccan Arabic jokes you might otherwise miss in *Humor and Moroccan Culture*, a wry account by American expat Mathew Helmke.

*Lords of the Atlas* by English historian Gavin Maxwell tells the true story of the vertiginous rise and prayers-answered fall of the notorious Thami el-Glaoui clan.

*The Sand Child* is the prize-winning novel about a girl raised as a boy by her father in Marrakesh by Fez-born author and psychotherapist Tahar ben Jelloun.

*Welcome to Paradise* is Marrakshi Mahi Binebine's breakthrough novel about a smuggler and an accidental fellowship of would-be Moroccan emigrants.

*The World's Embrace: Selected Poems* is a collection of poems by Abdel-latif Laâbi, founder of *Anfas/Souffles [Breaths]*, the free-form, free-thinking poetry magazine that landed Laâbi eight years in prison for 'crimes of opinion'. Government censorship notwithstanding, the complete French text of *Anfas/Souffles* is available online at http://clicnet.swarthmore .edu/souffles/sommaire.html.

# FILMS

To find out what Moroccan movies are showing next, check out the programme for Morocco's privately run culture channel at www.2M.tv. Look also for the following films in video stores and film festivals near you.

*The Man Who Knew Too Much* is Hitchcock's 1956 suspense classic about holidaymakers in Morocco accidentally foiling an assassination plot. Hitch plays up Marrakesh's mystique for maximum drama.

Farida ben Lyzaid's 1989 film *A Door to the Sky* tells the story of an émigré's return to Morocco, and her delicate balancing act between activism and tradition.

Bernardo Bertolucci's Golden Globe–winning 1990 epic *The Sheltering Sky* is based on Paul Bowles' breakthrough novel. The film co-stars John Malkovich and Debra Winger as hedonist-protagonists, and southern Morocco as itself.

*Les Yeux Secs* (Cry No More) is Narjiss Nejjar's controversial 2003 feature about a former prostitute who returns to her Berber village to stop her daughter from being drawn into the local flesh trade. The film won awards at both the Paris and Marrakesh film festivals.

Jilali Ferhati's 2004 film *Mémoires en Détention* (Memories in Detention) is about an ex-con's efforts to track down relatives of an inmate who lost his memory during his long detention.

Franco-Moroccan director Leila Marrakchi was awarded 'Un Certain Regard' at the 2005 Cannes Film Festival for her first feature *Marock*, about a Muslim girl and Jewish boy who fall in love.

# DIRECTORY
## TRANSPORT
### ARRIVAL & DEPARTURE
#### AIR

The main point of arrival and departure is **Menara airport** ( ☎ 024 447865), a 6km ride southwest of the Medina and Guéliz. *Petits taxis* (local taxis) cost Dh60 by day or Dh80 at night, or an airport transfer arranged through your riad (guesthouse) or hotel will be Dh150 to Dh200. Airport transfers to/from the Palmeraie cost Dh150 to Dh250.

If this is your first time at the hotel or riad in the Medina, arrange an airport transfer to deliver you to your destination so you don't get lost. Go with the airport-transfer option to the Palmeraie, as many taxi drivers are unfamiliar with Palmeraie roads. Hotels in Guéliz are easy to access by *petit taxi*.

Low-cost airlines are a benefit to travellers, but a burden on the environment and Marrakesh's air quality; to travel with a cleaner conscience, consider a carbon-offset programme (see p161) and a donation to a local nonprofit (p157).

#### Airport Information
**Flight information** ( ☎ 024 447865)
**Information desk** ( ☼ 8am-6pm)
**Royal Air Maroc** (Map pp38-9, D3; ☎ 024 436205; www.royalairmaroc.com; 197 Ave Mohammed V, Guéliz; ☼ 8.30am-12.30pm & 2.30-7pm)

## Transport Times

| | Djemaa el-Fna | Bab Laksour/ Mouassine | Rue de la Liberté | Bahia Palace | Kasbah/ Saadian Tombs | Jardin Majorelle |
|---|---|---|---|---|---|---|
| **Djemaa el-Fna** | n/a | walk 10min | taxi 5min | walk 15min | walk 20min | taxi 15min |
| **Bab Laksour/ Mouassine** | walk 10min | n/a | taxi 5min | taxi 5min | taxi 5min | taxi 10min |
| **Rue de la Liberté** | taxi 5min | taxi 5min | n/a | taxi 10min | taxi 10min | taxi 5min |
| **Bahia Palace** | walk 15min | taxi 5min | taxi 10min | n/a | walk 5min | taxi 15min |
| **Kasbah/ Saadian Tombs** | walk 20min | taxi 5min | taxi 10min | walk 5min | n/a | taxi 20min |
| **Jardin Majorelle** | taxi 15min | taxi 10min | taxi 5min | taxi 15min | taxi 20min | n/a |

## TRAIN

Trains run by the **Office National des Chemins de Fer** (ONCF; ☎ 024 447768) are convenient and inexpensive. Bookings to Casablanca and beyond can be made at the **main train station** (Map pp38-9, B4; cnr Ave Hassan II & Ave Mohammed VI) or through your riad or hotel.

## BUS

**Supratours** (Map pp38-9, A5; ☎ 024 435525; Ave Hassan II) offers cushy air-con buses to/from Essaouira and Agadir; book in person or via your hotel/riad. Book buses to/from Fez, Azilal/Cascades d'Ouzoud, Ouarzazate and other Moroccan cities at the CTM counter at Gare Routière (Map p91, A1) in Bab Doukkala, or at the **Guéliz CTM office** (Map pp38-9, B3; ☎ 024 448328; www.ctm .co.ma; Blvd Mohammed Zerktouni, Guéliz). Buses arrive and depart at Gare Routière.

## CUSTOMS & DUTY FREE

You can import the following into Morocco without customs duty: 200 cigarettes, 50 cigars or 400g of tobacco; 1L of spirits and 1L of wine; 5g of perfume; and unlimited amounts of foreign currency (amounts over Dh15,000 must be declared).

## LEFT LUGGAGE

Lockers with padlocks cost Dh10 per day at the main train station or Dh8 per day at Gare Routière; take valuables with you.

## TRAVEL DOCUMENTS

A current passport is required for entry to Morocco, and should be valid for at least six months from the date of entry. Entry may be refused to those with a 'hippie' appearance, so arrive neatly dressed to impress customs officers.

## VISA

No visas are necessary for visits under three months for citizens of the UK, USA, Canada, Australia, New Zealand and most Western European countries. South African visitors must have a valid visa from the Moroccan embassy in Pretoria.

## RETURN TICKET

A return ticket is required for travellers to Morocco.

## GETTING AROUND

Your feet are the best way to get around the Medina, which is mostly closed to car traffic. Driving in Marrakesh is an extreme sport, with scooters zooming from all sides and roundabouts the meek may never escape from – best to leave the driving to unfazed taxi drivers whenever possible. For day trips, you might rent a bike, car or a motorcycle.

## BUS

You can't miss the red double-decker buses of **Marrakech-Tour** ( ☎ 024 339637; www.marrakech-tour.com; adult/child day pass Dh130/65, 48hr pass Dh200/100; ⏰ every 30min from designated stops), which do a circuit of major Marrakesh landmarks and allow you to get on and off where you please. Check out the Medina and Guéliz with the 'Marrakesh Monumental' tour, or head to the Palmeraie on the 'Marrakesh Romantique' bus.

Public buses leave for the Nouvelle Ville at seemingly random intervals from Place de la Foucauld and cost Dh3. Key bus lines:

**Nos 1 & 20** Medina–Guéliz (along Ave Mohammed V).

**Nos 2 and 10** Medina–Gare Routière.

**Nos 3 and 8** Medina–train station.

**No 11** Medina–Menara Gardens.

## TAXI

### Petit Taxi

These beige compact taxis charge Dh5 to Dh15 by day for trips within Marrakesh, and slightly more at night. Check that the meter under the dash is on and at zero by day, Dh2.40 at night. Don't bother haggling if the meter is broken; anywhere in town should cost Dh15 max by day, or Dh25 at night.

Prime spots to catch *petit taxis* in the Medina: Gare Routière in Bab Doukkala; Bab Laksour in Mouassine; Bab er-Rob in the Kasbah; the corner of Rue el-Koutoubia and Ave Mohammed V, opposite Koutoubia Minaret, and Ave Houmman el-Fetouaki, near Rue Bab Agnaou, in Djemaa el-Fna.

In Nouvelle Ville, you'll find that the train station, the corner of Blvd Mohammed Zerktouni and Ave Mohammed V, Place de la Liberté, Place 16 Novembre, and Rue Echouhada in Hivernage are good taxi pick-up spots.

### Grand Taxi

These are fancy Mercedes you'll see near *petit taxi* stops and major hotels. They have no meters, and

---

### CLIMATE CHANGE & TRAVEL

Travel – especially air travel – is a significant contributor to global climate change. At Lonely Planet, we believe that all travellers have a responsibility to limit their personal impact. As a result, we have teamed with Rough Guides and other concerned industry partners to support Climate Care, which allows travellers to offset the greenhouse gases they are responsible for with contributions to energy-saving projects and other climate-friendly initiatives in the developing world. Lonely Planet offsets all staff and author travel.

For more information, turn to the responsible travel pages on www.lonely planet.com. For details on offsetting your carbon emissions and a carbon calculator, go to www.climatecare.org.

cost more than *petits taxis* after much haggling, but they'll take up to six people to out-of-town destinations. You can rent them in exclusivity for Essaouira for about Dh350, the Cascades d'Ouzoud for a little less, and Ourika for between Dh150 and Dh250.

## CALÈCHES

These are the horse-drawn green carriages you'll see at Place de la Foucauld next to the Djemaa el-Fna. One-way trips within the Medina cost Dh15; otherwise, state-fixed rates of Dh100 per hour apply. Expect a tour of the ramparts to take 1½ hours, and allow three hours for the Palmeraie. In the Hivernage, calèches linger outside major hotels along Ave el-Qadissia and Rue Echouhada.

## CAR & MOTORCYCLE RENTALS

Rates for car rentals range from Dh400 (from local agencies) to Dh600-plus (from multinational chains) per day; 4WDs cost Dh700 to Dh1000 with minimal insurance. An extra Dh150 to Dh250 could get you a driver, though English-speaking drivers aren't always available.

### Local Agencies

**Concorde Car** (Map pp38-9, B7; ☎ 024 431116; http://concordecar.ifrance.com; 154 Ave Mohammed V)

**KAT** (Map pp38-9, B7; ☎ 024 430175; 68 Blvd Mohammed Zerktouni; http://membres.lycos.fr/katcar)
**Lhasnaoui Rent** (Map pp38-9, F1; ☎ 070 959562; cnr Ave Allal el-Fassi & Yacoub el-Mansour)
**National** (www.nationalcar.com) Guéliz (Map pp38-9, B7; ☎ 024 430683; 1 Rue de la Liberté); airport ( ☎ 024 437846)

### Multinationals

**Avis** (www.avis.com) Guéliz (Map pp38-9, B8; ☎ 024 432525; 137 Ave Mohammed V); airport ( ☎ 024 433169)
**Budget** (www.budget.com) Guéliz (Map pp38-9, C2; ☎ 024 431180; 80 Blvd Mohammed Zerktouni; Mamounia Hotel ( ☎ 024 440720; Bab el-Jedid); airport ( ☎ 024 438875)
**Hertz** (www.hertz.com) Guéliz (Map pp38-9, B7; ☎ 024 439984; 154 Ave Mohammed V); airport ( ☎ 024 447230)

# PRACTICALITIES

## BUSINESS HOURS

Hours during summer and Ramadan may vary, but opening hours are usually:
**Banks** 8.30am to 12.30pm and 3pm to 6.30pm Monday to Thursday; 8.30am to noon and 3pm to 6.30pm Friday.
**Nouvelle Ville** 9.30am to 1.30pm and 3.30pm to 7.30pm Monday to Saturday.
**Medina** most 10am to 7pm (some close Friday afternoon and/or Sunday).

## CLIMATE & WHEN TO GO

A New Year or Easter holiday in Marrakesh might sound fun, but everyone else has the same idea. Hotels and riads raise their prices and flights are booked well in advance. For better rates and service, plan around these holidays.

Weather-wise, the best times to go are spring and autumn, when temperatures are 20°C to 25°C by day and at least 10°C by night, and November to February, when nights are cooler but similar daytime temperatures and light rainfall are possible.

The weather in March and April features sporadic, light rainfall with some sandstorms in April, while June sees dusty siroccos (desert winds) sweep through the city. From mid-June to August temperatures rise into the 30s and occasionally 40s.

## ELECTRICITY

**Voltage** 220V.
**Frequency** 50Hz.
**Cycle** AC.
**Plugs** Two round pins.

## EMERGENCIES

Crime and hustling is actively prevented by the *brigade touristique* (plain-clothes police officers) and locals keeping an eye on their neighbourhoods.

Main streets are relatively safe to walk along even at night, though be wary in dark alleys and mind your wallet as you would anywhere.

## EMERGENCY TELEPHONE NUMBERS

**Brigade Touristique** ( ☎ 024 384601)
**Fire** ( ☎ 15)
**Police** ( ☎ 19)
**Polyclinique du Sud** (private hospital; Map p38-9, B2; ☎ 024 447999)

## HEALTH
### IMMUNISATIONS

None are strictly necessary for Morocco, although hepatitis vaccinations and a tetanus booster are good safeguards.

### PRECAUTIONS

The main complaints visitors have in Marrakesh are stomach upset, dehydration and minor skin irritations, most of which can be avoided. Drink plenty of water to avoid dehydration and bring antidiarrhoeal pills to avoid pasha's revenge. Tap water is potable but can take some getting used to, so go for the bottled stuff. With lavish five-course Moroccan dinners, pace yourself and stick to small portions. Steer clear of food stalls with less-than-fresh oil or ingredients, and avoid juice and snack vendors who rinse and reuse drinking glasses or utensils. Sunblock is a must year-round, and powder prevents heat rashes.

### MEDICAL SERVICES

Travel insurance is advisable to cover any medical treatment in

Marrakesh; Morocco does not have reciprocal health-care arrangements with other countries. Basic care is inexpensive and can be found at hotel clinics during the day. Emergency medical care is available 24/7 at the **Polyclinique du Sud** (Map p38-9, B2; ☎ 024 447999; cnr Rue de Yougoslavie & Rue ibn Aicha). Patients with serious illnesses should fly home to see their own physicians.

## DENTAL SERVICES
Emergency dental care can be found at the Polyclinique du Sud and from English-speaking **Dr Bennani** (Map pp38-9, A7; ☎ 024 431145; 112 Ave Mohammed V).

## PHARMACIES
These are clearly marked with a green cross. In the Djemaa el-Fna there's a **late-night pharmacy** (Map p69, B4; ☎ 024 430415); others take turns as *pharmacies du garde* that open until midnight and on weekends – check listings posted on pharmacy doors and windows. After midnight, medications are available at the Polyclinique du Sud. Pharmacie Koutoubia (p93) offers European homeopathic remedies as well as pharmaceuticals.

## HOLIDAYS
State holidays are held on the same date each year, but religious holidays fall on different dates each year in accordance with the lunar Hejira calendar (which is 11 days shorter than the Gregorian calendar used in the UK and elsewhere). Public holidays for 2008 and 2009:

**New Year's Day** 1 January
**Fatih Muharram** (Muslim New Year) 10 January 2008, 29 December 2008
**Jan Manifesto of Independence** 11 January
**Aïd al-Mawlid** (Prophet's Birthday) 20 March 2008, 9 March 2009
**Labour Day** 1 May
**Feast of the Throne** 30 July
**Fête Oued Eddaha** (Oued Eddahab Allegiance Day) 14 August
**Révolution du Roi et du Peuple** (Anniversary of the King and the People's Revolution) 20 August
**King Mohammed's Birthday** 21 August
**Aïd al-Fitr** (End of Ramadan) 2 October 2008, 21 September 2009
**Marche Verte** (Anniversary of the Green March) 6 November
**Fête de l'Indépendance** (Independence Day) 18 November
**Aïd al-Adha** (Feast of the Sacrifice) 9 December 2008, 28 November 2009

Several hotels and riads offer wi-fi or computers with internet access. Otherwise, internet cafés ringing the Djemaa el-Fna are inexpensive (Dh8 to Dh12 per hour) and filled with locals flirting online. Most open by 10am and close around 11pm.

The main trouble-shooter in town for computer trouble is

**KNK La Kasbah Numérik** (Map p38-9, E2; ☎ 024 434568; www.lakasbah-numerik .com; Ave du Prince Moulay Abdullah).

## INTERNET CAFÉS

**Askmy Café** (Map pp38-9, B3; ☎ 024 430602; 6 Blvd Mohammed Zerktouni, Guéliz; ⏰ 8am-3am) Lickety-split connections on 14 terminals.

**Cyber Bab Agnaou** (Map p69, B6; Rue Bab Agnaou; ⏰ 9am-11pm) A dozen computers, with decent printers and scanners, downstairs in a shopping mall.

**Cyber Café in Cyberpark** (Map pp38-9, F5; off Ave Mohammed V; ⏰ 9.30am-7.30pm) Go figure: 15 terminals with fast connections in a royal rose garden.

## USEFUL WEBSITES

Lonely Planet's own website, www.lonelyplanet.com, offers a speedy link to many websites on Morocco. See p132 for accommodation websites; other handy Marrakesh sites include the following:

**Al-Bab** (www.al-bab.com/maroc/trav/marra kesh.htm) Gateway to Marrakesh, covering current affairs, news and books about Morocco.

**Amazigh Voice** (www.amazigh-voice.com) Online Berber Pride forum, with articles on Berber culture, language and heritage in French and English.

**Maghreb Arts** (www.maghrebarts.ma) French-language coverage of Moroccan film, music, theatre, art exhibitions and other cultural events.

**Maghreb Press** (www.map.ma/eng) The latest official news from Morocco in English.

**Moorish Girl** (www.lailalalami.com/blog) Insightful, topical blog by novelist Laila

Lalami (who wrote *Hope and Other Dangerous Pursuits*) about Moroccan culture and politics.

**Speak Moroccan** (www.speakmoroccan.com) A helpful website to pick up key phrases in Darija (Moroccan Arabic).

## LANGUAGE

In Marrakesh, you'll hear six main languages spoken: Tashelhit (a local Berber dialect), Darija (Moroccan dialect Arabic), French, Fusha (classical Arabic), Spanish and English. For key phrases in Darija and Tashelhit, see p82 and p73.

## MONEY

For current exchange rates, see the inside front cover, but here are some key figures to factor into your travel budget: a tagine costs Dh25-plus; bottled water Dh3 to Dh6; an overnight stay in a riad Dh350-plus; a spa treatment at a public hammam Dh30 to Dh50.

## TELEPHONE

Many European mobile phones work with Morocco's two GSM mobile-phone networks, but check with your carrier about roaming charges. Téléboutiques that sell phone cards and provide phone booths can be found all over town.

## COUNTRY & CITY CODES

For international calls from Morocco, dial ☎ 00 then the country code, the area code and the number. Morocco's country code is ☎ 212, followed by the area code minus the initial 0. Dial the ☎ 024 area code even if you're calling from within Marrakesh. Mobile numbers often begin with 061 or 068.

### USEFUL PHONE NUMBERS
**International operator** ( ☎ 120)
**Local directory inquiries** ( ☎ 160) If your French isn't so slick, ask your front desk clerk for help.

## TIPPING
Tipping is not only customary here, it's the bulk of many Marrakshi livelihoods. Tip waiters 10% to 15%, and leave a little something (Dh20 or so) for the riad staff who clean your room. In taxis, round up to the nearest dirham on the meter.

## TOURIST INFORMATION
The **Office National du Tourisme Marocain** ( Tourist Information Office; Map pp38-9,

A7; ☎ 024 436179; Place Abdel Moumen ben Ali, cnr Blvd Mohammed Zerktouni & Ave Mohammed V, Guéliz) is good for pamphlets and numbers of licensed guides, but not much else. For recommendations of where to go, ask at the place you're staying or talk to fellow travellers.

## TRAVELLERS WITH DISABILITIES
Overall, Marrakesh gets a poor rating for accessibility, though this hasn't deterred a growing number of intrepid disabled travellers. Wheelchair access is only provided in a few hotels, and navigating rutted alleys and crowded souqs is difficult. The lack of traffic signals and right-of-way are dangers for those with sight, hearing or mobility impairments.

However, some notable attractions, along with restaurants and gardens, are accessible to disabled travellers, and Marrakshis do their utmost to accommodate all guests.

# >INDEX

*See also separate subindexes for See (p173), Shop (p173), Eat (p174), Drink (p175) and Play (p175).*

**000** map pages

## 🍴 EAT

**000** map pages